THE TRIATHLETE'S GUIDE TO

Off-Season
Training

THE ULTRAFIT
MULTISPORT
TRAINING SERIES

Recently Published:

Going Long: Training for Ironman-Distance Triathlons, Joe Friel
    and Gordon Byrn

The Triathlete's Guide to Bike Training, Lynda Wallenfels

The Triathlete's Guide to Off-Season Training, Karen Buxton

Available Spring 2005:

The Triathlete's Guide to Run Training, Ken Mierke

The Triathlete's Guide to Swim Training, Stephen Tarpinian

Available Fall 2005:

*The Triathlete's Guide to Long-Distance Training: Half-Ironman
    Triathlons*, Tom Rogers

The Triathlete's Guide to Mental Training, Jim Taylor, Ph.D.

The Duathlete's Guide to Training and Racing, Eric Schwartz

Available Spring 2006:

The Triathlete's Guide to Sprint Distance Training, Gary Bredehoft

Off-Season Training

Karen Buxton

VELO press

Boulder, Colorado

The Triathlete's Guide to Off-Season Training

© 2004 Karen E. M. Buxton

Foreword © 2004 Joe Friel

Before embarking on any strenuous exercise program, including the training described in this book, everyone, particularly anyone with a known heart or blood pressure problem, should be examined by a physician.

Printed in the United States of America.

10 9 8 7 6 5 4 3 2 1

Distributed in the United States and Canada by Publishers Group West.

Library of Congress Cataloging-in-Publication Data

Buxton, Karen E. M.

   The triathlete's guide to off-season training / Karen E. M. Buxton.

      p. cm. — (Ultrafit multisport training series)

   Includes bibliographical references and index.

   ISBN 1-931382-51-4 (paperback : alk. paper)

      1. Triathlon—Training. 2. Physical fitness. I. Title. II. Series.

   GV1060.73.B88 2004

   796.42'57—dc22

2004011951

VeloPress®

1830 North 55th Street

Boulder, Colorado 80301–2700 USA

303/440-0601 • Fax 303/444-6788 • E-mail velopress@insideinc.com

To purchase additional copies of this book or other VeloPress® books, call 800/234-8356 or visit us on the Web at velopress.com.

Cover design by Rebecca Finkel, F + P Graphic Design, Inc.

Interior design by Rebecca Finkel, F + P Graphic Design, Inc., and Graphic Advantage, Ltd.

Swim photos (Chapter 5) are courtesy of Andy Hitchcock, Storyteller Productions. Photo 9.1 (page 128) by Casey B. Gibson. All other photos were provided by the author.

Spinner® and Spinning® are registered trademarks of Mad Dog Athletics, Inc.

To my brother Jeff —
Your continued strength, spirit, and good
humor through all that you've faced is an
inspiration. Thank you.

Contents

Acknowledgments

I must first thank my husband, Terry, and my children, Marty and Elizabeth, for their never-ending love and support. Also, words cannot express my gratitude to my at-home editor and sounding board, Terry, who now knows more about off-season triathlon training than he could ever imagine.

I would also like to thank Joe Friel, my mentor and business associate, who provided me with the opportunity to create this book and Amy Rinehart and VeloPress for supporting me through the process and overseeing the publishing of this manuscript.

Foreword

Ask multisport coaches what the most important part of the training year is and most will say winter. Why is this? Winter is when the athlete establishes the base of fitness that will ultimately determine race fitness later in the season. This is nothing new. There's an old saying that the broader the base is, the higher the peak will be. The question isn't whether or not to follow a calculated training system in the off-season, but how.

In the following pages, Karen Buxton tells you exactly how to create optimal base fitness during the important winter months. The training system she describes is what Karen and many other coaches have found to be successful in preparing their athletes for the eventual rigors of high-performance training that follows in the spring and summer. Follow the guidelines offered here, and you are well on your way to an excellent season.

I asked Karen to write this book because she is a master coach who has been at it a long time. In fact, Karen was one of the first coaches I selected to join my company, Ultrafit Associates. Back in the year 2000, she became our fourth associate and helped to train and serve as a role model for many of the coaches who subsequently joined us. Our coaches go through a rigorous selection process and then are thoroughly trained to use the *Training Bible* system of coaching. Those who become associates are among the best in the sport.

Karen is a rock-solid coach who has a firm grasp on what it takes to be successful as an athlete. She has proven this with her own success as a multisport athlete and with the many successful athletes she has coached over the years. Carefully read and implement what she offers here, and you can also create the kind of fitness that produces high-performance peaks in the coming season.

JOE FRIEL
ULTRAFIT SERIES EDITOR

1

The Importance of the Off-Season:

BACKING OFF WITH A PURPOSE

THE TRANSITION PHASE

For the same reason that you should build rest days into a week of training and reduced-volume/rest weeks into your training cycles, you also need a longer rest phase (4 to 5 weeks) within your yearly cycle. This phase, called the "transition phase," leads your off-season, and it occurs immediately following your last competition and prior to the "base-building period." Often, an athlete will refrain from any type of activity during this phase and become the proverbial "couch potato." While a few complete days of rest can be beneficial, prolonged inactivity can lead to a dramatic loss of fitness.

Studies have shown that a complete cessation of training can cause between a 4 percent and 14 percent decrease in VO_2max (i.e., the capacity for oxygen consumption by the body during maximal exertion—also known as aerobic capacity and max oxygen consumption) in as little as 4 weeks. Endurance performance has also been shown to decrease as much as 25 percent during a period of 2 to 4 weeks of inactivity. Further studies have demonstrated negative changes in blood volume, lactate concentration, lactate threshold, muscle glycogen, capillary density, and mitochondrial volume. Thus, it is important to *decrease, not cease, your activity during your transition period.* This will allow you to maintain your fitness gains, so that you have a solid foundation to build upon going into the remainder of your off-season.

What should you be doing during your transition phase to prepare you for the upcoming "base phase"? Think of this transition phase as a time of unstructured training. You having been living by your training log all year, and now is the time to train when you want. The following list should help you to relax and recharge, while maintaining a general level of fitness.

- Lose the training log and relax.
- Throw in a day or two (or three) of complete rest.
- Stay off the road bike and hit the trails on the mountain bike.
- Stay off the roads and head to the running trails.
- Try deep-water running or an aqua-fitness class.
- Lock up the heart rate monitor and gauge your exertion by feel.
- Try something new like yoga or Pilates™.
- Take long walks with family, friends, or your pet.
- Head to the lake for a paddle in a kayak or canoe.
- Stay away from your master's swim group.
- Swim on your own and do not count the yardage.
- Skip the weight room and perform only body weight exercises.
- Sleep in.
- Sleep in.
- Sleep in.

Some athletes report feeling "funky" during this time of reduced training. This feeling is similar to the "taper funk" that often occurs when athletes back off from large volumes of training. In essence, your body is going through exercise withdrawal and needs to get used to the feeling of less exercise. Do not let this feeling cause you to cut short your transition period. This mental and physical break is a much-needed phase within your entire training plan and, if followed properly, will prepare your body and mind to begin your next phase of training with eagerness—the Base phase.

LOOKING BACK TO PLAN AHEAD

With your race season still fresh in your mind and the unstructured nature of your current training giving you some newly found time, the transition phase is perfect to start planning for your upcoming season. But, before you start to map out your annual training plan (ATP), you need to look back at this past season's goals, objectives, training schedule, and race results. You need to assess the past before you plan for the future, and asking yourself the following questions will help you shape your training plans for the upcoming season.

Did you meet your goals?
Did you follow your training objectives?
Did you address your limiters?
Were you able to stick to your training schedule?
Were you satisfied with your racing results?

When planning the upcoming season, think about how difficult or easy it was to meet your goals. Were they reasonable, too easily met, or well beyond your reach? Once you met a goal, did you set another? Did your training objectives lead you to your goals? Training objectives are the stepping-stones to your goals and must be followed closely. Your training objectives should focus on your limiters. (Did you determine these?) In order to improve performance, you must focus on your weaknesses while maintaining your strengths.

Looking back at your training journal, were you able to stick to your training schedule? You need to set your training hours to blend into your daily schedule. Do not set yourself up for failure by scheduling more hours than you have available to train. Did you feel good about your race results? Remember to think about your race effort, and do not compare yourself to your competition. Did your race schedule fit into your life schedule? Not having enough races in a season can lead to seemingly endless training, yet having too many races can lead to burnout. Balancing your race schedule with a good mixture of "A, B, and C level" races ("A" being the most important, "C" the least) will keep you motivated to train and eager to race.

Looking back at your season and evaluating the good and the bad results will provide you with a solid outline to begin designing your training plan for the upcoming season. Chapter 2 will provide you with some personal assessment forms that will help you pinpoint your strengths and weaknesses and determine what limiters you need to address to reach your goals.

The next step to a successful season is to design your off-season training plan. Remember, a varied and carefully planned off-season will provide you with the solid foundation that you will need to achieve your goals for the upcoming season. As you use the next chapter to design your off-season plan (Preparation, Base I, II, and III phases), you will define and set goals, determine limiters, and set appropriate training objectives. So, break out a pencil and paper and get ready to map out your road to results.

REFERENCES

Bergman, Bryan C. "Maintaining Training Adaptations During the Off-Season." www.ridefast.com/page.asp?page_id=content&page_content=A-8&CategoryID=66&ArticleID=27#article

Friel, Joe. *The Triathlete's Training Bible.* 2nd ed. Boulder, CO: VeloPress, 2004.

2 Goal-Setting:

MAPPING OUT THE ROAD TO RESULTS

This chapter will show you how to design your off-season training plan (OTP). Your OTP will be the stepping-stone to your upcoming season. The plan will become a portion of your annual training plan (ATP) by breaking the year (macrocycle) into smaller portions (microcycles). The microcycles that we will focus on are:

Preparation
Base I
Base II
Base III

SETTING YOUR GOALS

Before designing your OTP, you must first set your goals for the upcoming season. Chapter 1 discussed how to review your previous season and use that information to shape your upcoming season. Using this information, you are ready to write down your goals. However, if you are going to set goals, you should first know what constitutes an appropriate goal. The right kind of goal is one that provides direction and enhances motivation. It is very important to set attainable, yet challenging goals. You always want to stretch yourself to reach your goal. However, it is no fun if you cannot achieve your goals. Easy goals do not require enough discipline to make them count and thus result in low motivation and minimal satisfaction. By the same token, small and specific goals can yield big results. All of this, though, presupposes that you know where you are and where you are headed: "If you don't know where you're going, every road's the same."

At the end of each racing season, it is helpful to look back at your results and determine where you ranked against the field in each discipline. Triathlon and duathlon race results provide clear feedback for this calculation. If, for example, you find that your bike split is consistently slower against the field than your swim and run, then you can target cycling for specific attention in your training for the upcoming season. It is important to note here that this biking goal needs to be set in terms of your personal training focus (to build more strength on hills), not in terms of how you finished versus your competition (to make the top ten at nationals). For example, an athlete, Jim, focuses on improving his bike split, reasoning that this will propel him into the upper echelons of his age group. His hard work in the off-season pays off, and Jim realizes significant gains in his personal times. However, some of his competitors were apparently also looking to improve their bike splits and did so with better results than Jim's. Thus, Jim's overall standing in his age group did not improve as significantly as he had hoped. The lesson here is: You can only control your performance! The positive reality here is that this athlete's goal-setting resulted in appreciable improvements in his performance, which will bear even more fruit in the years to come.

Just as races are won or lost somewhere on the hills or windy flats in the middle of a competition, so seasons are made or broken in the specific daily workouts leading up to the first race. It is crucial to plan this preparation time carefully, since we don't all have endless hours to spend on training. Well-set goals help to keep us focused, so that we use our limited time more productively. The time that you spend now looking back and analyzing your past season will prove invaluable as you plan for the one ahead.

The first key point in effective goal-setting is to assess where you are, based on the past season's results. Once you have done that, it's time to map out a strategy for improvement: In other words, it is time to set your goals for the upcoming season. There are different types of goals you can set: performance-based (to set a personal best on the bike course at a race that you've done before) and practice-oriented (to swim 10 × 100s in 1 hr., 30 min.); long-term (to qualify for the Hawaii Ironman®) or short-term (to strength train 3 days next week); and physical (to build a solid aerobic base over the winter) or psychological (to have fun). All of these types of goals should be considered when designing your training and racing schedule.

Following is a list of nine principles to help you set your goals and get you on the road to a successful and purposeful season.

Goal-Setting Principles

Set specific goals.
Set difficult, but realistic goals.
Set long- and short-term goals.
Set performance goals.
Write down goals.
Develop strategies to achieve goals.
Be committed to your goals.
Get others to support you in your goals.
Develop tools to help you evaluate your progress toward goals.

Setting specific goals is much more beneficial than setting general goals. Saying that your goal is to do your best on the 40K bike leg of a triathlon is not as motivating as saying that your goal is to cut your best 40K bike time by 3 minutes. When setting specific goals, it is important that they be measurable ("by 3 minutes") and that they be explained in behavioral terms (working on pedaling technique in the off-season).

Goals should be challenging and difficult, but realistic enough to achieve. Setting our sights on making the Olympic team is not a realistic goal for most of us; but finishing in the top ten of a local sprint may be within reach. Easy goals that take little or no effort to achieve often mislead us to be satisfied by a mediocre performance. If an athlete does not stretch himself, he may never reach his potential or even understand what that potential might be. On the other hand, setting goals that are too difficult or unrealistic can lead to frustration, poor performance, and lowered self-confidence and motivation. As mentioned earlier, it is essential that you have a realistic understanding of your present abilities before you set any goals, whether you are a first-year athlete or in your tenth year of racing.

Setting long and short-term goals is like climbing a ladder—there are steps that you must take to reach the top. Each rung in the ladder represents an objective (short-term goal) that moves you toward the top (long-term goal). Achieving short-term goals along the way provides an athlete with more immediate and usable feedback, which makes the long-term goal more attainable. A long-term goal thus becomes the natural consequence of properly set and acted upon short-term goals. For example, setting a goal of swimming 100-yard repeats at a certain pace is a step to achieving your targeted time for the swim leg in a triathlon.

It is important to set goals based on your performance rather than that of others. You can only control how *you* train and prepare for your racing season. Your competition's preparation and development is completely out of your hands. You may "lose" to a competitor in a race while still setting a personal best. But if your sole goal was to beat the competitor, then your personal best will not be seen for the accomplishment that it is.

Once your goals are set, they should be written down in a place where they can be checked daily. Your training journal is the perfect place to do this. By having your long-term goal in front of you every day, you can focus on your daily and weekly training and racing goals, knowing they are taking you a step (or run) closer to the top. (Reminding myself in January that the 45-minute one-legged drill session on the bike is moving me toward my goal of a faster 40K bike split in June puts those workouts in perspective and makes them manageable.)

Strategies for achieving your goals are the road map to your training and racing season. For example, focusing on drill work as you swim during the off-season is a strategy to achieve a goal of lowering your 1.5K swim time by 1 minute. When setting your strategies to achieve goals, it is important to be flexible. Rather than saying that you will swim on Monday, Wednesday, and Friday, it is better to say that you will swim 3 days a week. If you have the flexibility to alter your schedule to fit your swim into it, you will still achieve your goals.

Goals are impossible to achieve without commitment. If you are going to take the time to map out your season, you need to be committed to each step of the process in pursuit of your goals. Staying focused on the direction in which you are heading and putting forth a solid effort are essential elements of that commitment.

Having the support of others (coach, spouse, training partners) is critical in helping you achieve your goals. Having a coach in your corner helps you sustain motivation and direction; a spouse or partner provides someone to share the challenges, frustrations, and accomplishments with; and training partners can help encourage you to leave the warmth of your house for that long run on a cold and wet winter's day.

Tools for evaluating your goals and your steps to achieving them are essential if goals are going to improve your performance. Once you have set your specific goals and mapped out your strategy, you need to have evaluation tools in place. For example, if one of your specific goals is to reduce your swim stroke count per 25 yards from 22 to 20, record your average stroke count from your daily workouts. If, over a period of time, the count is not decreasing, you can adjust your strategy to better achieve your goal (i.e., alter drill-sets to focus more on gliding). On the other hand, if you achieve your target stroke count, it is time to check off that goal and move on to another. Similarly, if you are injured and cannot train as scheduled, you need to reassess and set new goals that can be accomplished (i.e., deep-water running rather than regular running, if you have a stress fracture).

Setting goals helps us transform our desires into our reality; but worthwhile goals require discipline and dedication. Remember, "if wishes were horses, we'd all be riding." So in this off-season, break out the pencil and paper, jot down your goals, and map out your strategy (set specific training objectives) to achieve them. See Appendix A for a Goal-Setting Worksheet.

DETERMINING YOUR STRENGTHS, WEAKNESSES, AND LIMITERS

Now that you have set your goals, you need to think about what you must do to achieve them. Another way of understanding this is to ask: What is holding you back from attaining your goals? All athletes have strengths and weaknesses, and in training, successful athletes maintain their strengths while overcoming their weaknesses. So how do you determine what you are good at and what your shortcomings are? You need to step back and do some honest self-appraisal. First, complete the three assessment forms found in this chapter: the Triathlete Proficiency Scale, the Triathlete Natural Abilities Profile, and the Triathlon Assessment. Answer the questions within honestly, as the results will be the basis of the design for your upcoming training plan.

This first form, the Triathlete Proficiency Scale, provides you with information relating to how you perform against others in your age group. Pull out your race results from this past season and see how you rank against the field in each of the three disciplines. You may see a poorer result versus the field in the swim leg as compared to the bike and run, and thus your swim can be considered a weakness. Or you may see that your bike ranking drops down on hilly courses, while the swim and run rankings remain consistent. In this case your bicycling on hilly courses becomes your weakness, and thus climbing (force) is a limiter for you on the bike. By determining where your weaknesses lie, you can best focus on what you need to improve on during the off-season, which will bring you one step closer to reaching your goals.

Your success in multisport is dependent upon three basic abilities: *endurance,* which is the ability to delay the onset of fatigue; *force,* which is the ability to use your muscles to overcome resistance; and *speed,* which is the ability to move efficiently (efficient movement equals speed). The second form, Triathlete Natural Abilities Profile, will help you determine where your strengths and weaknesses lie within the three multisport disciplines.

TRIATHLETE PROFICIENCY SCALE

Compared with those in my age group, I am among the . . .

SPORT	WORST		AVERAGE		BEST
Swimming	1	2	3	4	5
Cycling	1	2	3	4	5
Running	1	2	3	4	5

Source: *The Triathlete's Training Bible* by Joe Friel (Boulder, CO: VeloPress, 2004).

TRIATHLETE NATURAL ABILITIES PROFILE

Read each statement below and decide if you agree or disagree as it applies to you. Check the appropriate answer. If unsure, go with your initial feeling.

A   D   A=AGREE   D=DISAGREE

____ ____ 1. I prefer to ride in a bigger gear with a lower cadence than most of my training partners.

____ ____ 2. The shorter the race, the better I perform.

____ ____ 3. As the intervals get shorter, I get better.

____ ____ 4. I'm stronger at the end of long workouts than my training partners.

____ ____ 5. I can squat and/or leg press more weight than most in my category.

____ ____ 6. I prefer long races.

____ ____ 7. I run and bike in the hills better than most in my age group.

____ ____ 8. I enjoy high-volume training weeks.

____ ____ 9. My running stride is short and quick.

____ ____ 10. I have always been better at sprints than at endurance races.

____ ____ 11. In most sports, I've finish stronger than most others.

____ ____ 12. I'm more muscular than most multisport athletes of my age and sex.

____ ____ 13. I'm better at swimming in rough water than most others in my age group.

____ ____ 14. I prefer workouts that are short, but fast.

____ ____ 15. I'm confident of my endurance at the start of long races.

Scoring: For each of the following sets of statements, count the number of "Agree" answers you checked.

Statement numbers

1, 5, 7, 12, 13: Number of "Agrees" _____ Force score

2, 3, 9, 10, 14: Number of "Agrees" _____ Speed score

4, 6, 8, 11, 15: Number of "Agrees" _____ Endurance score

Source: *The Triathlete's Training Bible,* 2nd ed., by Joe Friel (Boulder, CO: VeloPress, 2004).

TRIATHLON ASSESSMENT

Score each of the following racing abilities and miscellaneous factors on a scale of 1–5 using the following guidelines. Circle the selection that best describes you in relation to your competition.

1 = among the worst in my age group/bad
3 = average in my age group/average
5 = among the best in my age group/excellent

ABILITIES/TECHNIQUES	SWIM	BIKE	RUN
Endurance	1 2 3 4 5	1 2 3 4 5	1 2 3 4 5
Force	1 2 3 4 5	1 2 3 4 5	1 2 3 4 5
Speed	1 2 3 4 5	1 2 3 4 5	1 2 3 4 5
Muscular endurance	1 2 3 4 5	1 2 3 4 5	1 2 3 4 5
Anaerobic endurance	1 2 3 4 5	1 2 3 4 5	1 2 3 4 5
Power	1 2 3 4 5	1 2 3 4 5	1 2 3 4 5
Technique	1 2 3 4 5	1 2 3 4 5	1 2 3 4 5

Miscellaneous Factors

	SWIM	BIKE	RUN
Time to train	1 2 3 4 5	1 2 3 4 5	1 2 3 4 5
Injuries	1 2 3 4 5	1 2 3 4 5	1 2 3 4 5
Health	1 2 3 4 5	1 2 3 4 5	1 2 3 4 5
Body strength	1 2 3 4 5	1 2 3 4 5	1 2 3 4 5
Flexibility	1 2 3 4 5	1 2 3 4 5	1 2 3 4 5
Mental skills	1 2 3 4 5	1 2 3 4 5	1 2 3 4 5
Nutrition	1 2 3 4 5	1 2 3 4 5	1 2 3 4 5
Body composition	1 2 3 4 5	1 2 3 4 5	1 2 3 4 5

Source: *The Triathlete's Training Bible*, 2nd ed., by Joe Friel (Boulder, CO: VeloPress, 2004).

Depending upon the distance of your event, each of the three abilities plays a role in your individual success. Endurance is the foundation of success for all distances in multisport racing, from sprint to iron distance. In the meantime, force can come into play on hilly courses or in rough open-water swims. And speed plays a large role in sprint distance races or close finishes in all distances—the ability to increase speed at the end of a race can be the difference between a qualifying spot for the Hawaii Ironman® or just finishing.

After filling out the Triathlete Natural Abilities Profile, tally the scores. If you scored four or five "Agrees" in the ability, you show strength in the designated area. A score of three or less demonstrates a weakness.

The final form is the Triathlon Assessment, which includes not only ability and proficiency limiters, but other outside factors that can inhibit your improvement. As with the Triathlete Natural Abilities Profile, fours and fives indicate a strength or a positive in that particular area, and threes or below highlight a weakness or a limiter.

Now that you have completed these forms, how can you best utilize the analysis of your answers to help build your plan for the off-season? Let's do a quick review of what you have mapped out so far. You have:

- Taken a bit of unstructured training time to refresh your body and mind;
- Evaluated your past season;
- Written down appropriate goals for the upcoming season;
- Determined your current strengths and weaknesses;
- Identified your limiter(s).

The next step is to write down your training objectives—the stepping-stones to your goals. Training objectives are specific smaller goals that you use in your training plan to improve your limiters. Go to your goal-setting worksheet that you have already filled out, read your first goal, and ask yourself if any of the weaknesses that you have now identified is a limiter for that specific goal. If so, you need to create training objectives that will turn that limiter into one of your strengths. Complete the same steps with each goal that you have listed.

The following examples illustrate appropriate goals, specific limiters, and measurable training objectives.

OLYMPIC-DISTANCE SAMPLE GOAL

Goal: Break 23 minutes for a 1.5K open-water swim at St. Anthony's Triathlon in April

Limiter: Swim technique

Training Objectives:

1. Participate in a masters swim group at least two times per week during the off-season and swim at least two additional sessions per week.

2. Build to five swim sessions per week by the first of March.

3. Incorporate drill sets in every swimming workout throughout the off-season and racing season.

4. Attend a weekend swim camp in January.

Observations:

- Breaking 23 minutes is an appropriate goal since the athlete swam 24:10 last year at St. Anthony's.

- Swim technique is a specific limiter because the athlete neglected drill work in the previous season.

- Each objective is measurable because it has a time frame associated with it—"five times per week, by the first of March, in January . . ."

DESIGNING YOUR OFF-SEASON TRAINING SCHEDULE

Now that you have set your goals, identified your current limiters, and set your training objectives, it is time to map out your training plan for your off-season. The first step is to determine the number of available hours you have for training. Your log from last season (again, looking back to plan ahead) should help you determine this.

Add up your total number of hours that you have trained over the past twelve months. If you are thinking about advancing to a longer-distance race this year and your daily schedule can handle the increase,

HALF-IRONMAN–DISTANCE SAMPLE GOAL

Goal: Run a 1 hour, 40 minutes or better marathon at the Blackwater Eagleman Half-Ironman® in June

Limiter: Running endurance off the bike

Training Objectives:

1. Complete 6 × 1-mile repeats of 6 minutes, 45 seconds each with a 400-walk/jog recovery by March 30.

2. Build run frequency to six times per week by April 1.

3. Build long run off the bike to 2 hours (at a 7 minute, 45-second-per mile pace) by April 20.

4. Run 1 hour, 35 minutes or better at the half-marathon on May 1.

Observations:

- Running 1 hour, 35 minutes is an appropriate goal since the athlete ran 1 hour, 40 minutes at a marathon at the end of his last season.

- Running endurance off the bike is a specific limiter since the longest run the athlete did off the bike last year was 1 hour, 30 minutes.

- Each objective has a time frame for completion and is measurable.

it is then appropriate to increase your volume by 10 to 15 percent. Or if your "life" schedule has changed (new job, children, or the addition of other commitments), you may need to reduce your number of training hours. But, if you are sticking to the same racing plan and you are comfortable with your current training hours, do not change your volume.

If you have not kept current with your training log or have trained by distance rather than time, you will have to estimate your time per week. One way to do this is to take your highest volume week (total number of training hours) and look at Table 2.1 and find the Base III, week 3 row. Locate the hours closest to your highest training week and

2.1 WEEKLY TRAINING HOURS: BASE AND PREP PHASES

PERIOD	WEEK	ANNUAL HOURS					
		200	250	300	350	400	450
Prep	All	3.5	4.0	5.0	6.0	7.0	7.5
Base I	1	4.0	5.0	6.0	7.0	8.0	9.0
	2	5.0	6.0	7.0	8.5	9.5	10.5
	3	5.5	6.5	8.0	9.5	10.5	12.0
	4	3.0	3.5	4.0	5.0	5.5	6.5
Base II	1	4.0	5.5	6.5	7.5	8.5	9.5
	2	5.0	6.5	7.5	9.0	10.0	11.5
	3	5.5	7.0	8.5	10.0	11.0	12.5
	4	3.0	3.5	4.5	5.0	5.5	6.5
Base III	1	4.5	5.5	7.0	8.0	9.0	10.0
	2	5.0	6.5	8.0	9.5	10.5	12.0
	3	6.0	7.5	9.0	10.5	11.5	13.0
	4	3.0	3.5	4.5	5.0	5.5	6.5

Source: *The Triathlete's Training Bible,* 2nd ed., by Joe Friel (Boulder, CO: VeloPress, 2004).

follow that number up to the annual hours. For example, if your highest volume week was 15 hours (found in Base III, week 3 row) last year, you will have about 500 available hours to train.

If you have neglected to keep track of your past year's training altogether, you can use Table 2.2 (see page 18) as a guideline to get you started. Remember that these are just guidelines, and you want to choose the number of hours that best fits *your* lifestyle. It is always better to err on the light side of volume, rather than putting too much on your plate and risking setting yourself up for disappointment by not being able to carry out your prescribed workouts. You can always adjust the schedule upward as you move along. Once you have set your annual hours, go to the Off-Season Training Plan Worksheet found

ANNUAL HOURS									
500	**550**	**600**	**650**	**700**	**750**	**800**	**850**	**900**	**950**
8.5	9.0	10.0	11.0	12.0	12.5	13.5	14.5	15.0	16.0
10.0	11.0	12.0	12.5	14.0	14.5	15.5	16.5	17.5	18.5
12.0	13.0	14.5	15.5	16.5	18.0	19.0	20.0	21.0	21.5
13.5	14.5	16.0	17.5	18.5	20.0	21.5	22.5	24.0	25.5
7.0	8.0	8.5	9.0	1.0	10.5	11.5	12.0	12.5	13.5
10.5	12.5	12.5	13.0	14.5	16.0	17.0	18.0	19.0	20.0
12.5	14.0	15.0	16.5	17.5	19.0	20.0	21.5	22.5	24.0
14.0	15.5	17.0	18.0	19.5	21.0	22.5	24.0	25.0	26.5
7.0	8.0	9.0	10.0	10.5	11.5	12.0	12.5	13.5	14.0
11.0	12.5	13.5	14.5	15.5	17.0	18.0	19.0	20.0	21.0
13.5	14.5	16.0	17.0	18.5	20.0	21.5	23.0	24.0	25.0
15.0	16.5	18.0	19.0	20.5	22.0	23.5	25.0	26.5	28.0
7.0	8.0	8.5	9.0	10.0	10.5	11.5	12.0	12.5	13.5

in Appendix B and enter your hours. (Appendix C presents a sample worksheet filled in for an athlete who has 500 available annual training hours.)

The training cycles in this book will follow a 3-week "on," 1-week "off" pattern—that is, 3 weeks of progressively increased volume and intensity, followed by 1 week of decreased volume and intensity. You may choose to follow a 2-week "on," 1-week "off" pattern. This will depend upon many factors, including your age, ability to recover, time available to train, and more. You may need to experiment to discover which pattern works best for you. If in doubt, begin with the 2-weeks on, 1-week off pattern—it is always easier mentally and physically to add more training hours than to take them away. Once you

2.2 SUGGESTED ANNUAL TRAINING HOURS

RACE DISTANCE/CLASSIFICATION	ANNUAL HOURS
Ironman	600–1,200
Half-Ironman	500–700
International	400–600
Sprint	300–500
Juniors (16–19 years old) International and Sprint	200–350

have determined which weekly pattern you will follow, you can use Table 2.3 to help you set your daily training hours.

Prior to designing your plan, you will also need to look at your upcoming racing schedule so that when you create your off-season plan, it flows directly into the build phase of your racing season. You may need to extend or cut short your Preparation phase, or you can include double doses of any of the Base phases. If you are fairly new to triathlon, you may need to extend the Base I phase to establish a stronger aerobic base. If you need to develop greater muscular endurance, sport-specific strength, or are participating in a long-distance event, you can choose to repeat the Base II or III phase. You will need to tailor the adjustments to the your particular needs.

PREPARATION PHASE

Following your transition period, which should last from 2 to 6 weeks, you will need to include a short period of increased activity, called the Preparation phase. This phase begins the structured training portion of your off-season and, as the name implies, it prepares you for the upcoming increased rigors of your base period.

During the Preparation phase, which should last from 3 to 4 weeks, your main focus is to build your aerobic engine and improve your technique in all three disciplines. So, on your Off-Season Training Plan Worksheet (see Appendix B), under each discipline place an *X* under the Endurance and Speed abilities column. Since the main focus of this phase of your training is on improving your cardiorespiratory

2.3 DAILY TRAINING HOURS

(May be two-a-day workouts, or three-a-day for elites)

TOTAL WEEKLY HOURS	SUGGESTED DAILY HOURS						
	MON.	TUES.	WED.	THURS.	FRI.	SAT.	SUN.
3:00	1:30	0:45	0:45	Off	Off	Off	Off
3:30	1:30	1:00	1:00	Off	Off	Off	Off
4:00	1:30	1:00	1:00	0:30	Off	Off	Off
4:30	1:30	1:00	0:45	0:45	0:30	Off	Off
5:00	1:30	1:00	1:00	1:00	0:30	Off	Off
5:30	1:30	1:15	1:00	1:00	0:45	Off	Off
6:00	1:30	1:15	1:00	1:00	0:45	0:30	Off
6:30	1:30	1:15	1:00	1:00	1:00	0:45	Off
7:00	1:30	1:30	1:15	1:00	1:00	0:45	Off
7:30	2:00	1:30	1:15	1:00	1:00	0:45	Off
8:00	2:00	1:30	1:15	1:15	1:00	1:00	Off
8:30	2:00	1:30	1:15	1:15	1:00	1:00	0:30
9:00	2:00	1:30	1:30	1:15	1:00	1:00	0:45
9:30	2:30	1:30	1:30	1:15	1:00	1:00	0:45
10:00	2:30	2:00	1:30	1:15	1:00	1:00	0:45
10:30	2:30	2:00	1:30	1:30	1:00	1:00	1:00
11:00	2:30	2:00	1:30	1:30	1:30	1:00	1:00
11:30	3:00	2:00	1:30	1:30	1:30	1:00	1:00
12:00	3:00	2:00	2:00	1:30	1:30	1:00	1:00
12:30	3:30	2:00	2:00	1:30	1:30	1:00	1:00
13:00	3:30	2:30	2:00	1:30	1:30	1:00	1:00
13:30	3:30	2:30	2:00	2:00	1:30	1:00	1:00
14:00	4:00	2:30	2:00	2:00	1:30	1:00	1:00
14:30	4:00	2:30	2:00	2:00	1:30	1:30	1:00
15:00	4:00	2:30	2:30	2:00	1:30	1:30	1:00
15:30	4:00	2:30	2:30	2:00	2:00	1:30	1:00
16:00	4:00	3:00	2:30	2:00	2:00	1:30	1:00
16:30	4:00	3:00	2:30	2:30	2:00	1:30	1:00
17:00	4:00	3:00	2:30	2:30	2:00	2:00	1:00
17:30	4:30	3:00	2:30	2:30	2:00	2:00	1:00
18:00	4:30	3:00	3:00	2:30	2:00	2:00	1:00

2.3 (CONTINUED) DAILY TRAINING HOURS

TOTAL WEEKLY HOURS	SUGGESTED DAILY HOURS						
	MON.	TUES.	WED.	THURS.	FRI.	SAT.	SUN.
18:30	4:30	3:00	3:00	2:30	2:30	2:00	1:00
19:00	4:30	3:30	3:00	2:30	2:30	2:00	1:00
19:30	4:30	3:30	3:00	3:00	2:30	2:00	1:00
20:00	4:30	3:30	3:00	3:00	2:30	2:30	1:00
20:30	5:00	3:30	3:00	3:00	2:30	2:30	1:00
21:00	5:00	3:30	3:30	3:00	2:30	2:30	1:00
21:30	5:00	3:30	3:30	3:00	3:00	2:30	1:00
22:00	5:00	4:00	3:30	3:00	3:00	2:30	1:00
22:30	5:00	4:00	3:30	3:30	3:00	2:30	1:00
23:00	5:00	4:00	3:30	3:30	3:00	2:30	1:30
23:30	5:30	4:00	3:30	3:30	3:00	2:30	1:30
24:00	5:30	4:00	4:00	3:30	3:00	2:30	1:30
24:30	5:30	4:00	4:00	3:30	3:30	2:30	1:30
25:00	5:30	4:30	4:00	3:30	3:30	2:30	1:30
25:30	5:30	4:30	4:00	4:00	3:30	2:30	1:30
26:00	6:00	4:30	4:00	4:00	3:30	2:30	1:30
26:30	6:00	4:30	4:00	4:00	3:30	3:00	1:30
27:00	6:00	4:30	4:30	4:00	3:30	3:00	1:30
27:30	6:00	4:30	4:30	4:00	4:00	3:00	1:30
28:00	6:00	5:00	4:30	4:00	4:00	3:00	1:30
28:30	6:00	5:00	4:30	4:30	4:00	3:00	1:30
29:00	6:00	5:00	4:30	4:30	4:00	3:30	1:30
29:30	6:00	5:00	4:30	4:30	4:00	3:30	2:00
30:00	6:00	5:00	5:00	4:30	4:00	3:30	2:00
30:30	6:00	5:00	5:00	4:30	4:30	3:30	2:00
31:00	6:00	5:30	5:00	4:30	4:30	3:30	2:00
31:30	6:00	5:30	5:00	5:00	4:30	3:30	2:00
32:00	6:00	5:30	5:00	5:00	4:30	4:00	2:00
32:30	6:00	5:30	5:30	5:00	4:30	4:00	2:00
33:00	6:00	5:30	5:30	5:00	5:00	4:00	2:00
33:30	6:00	6:00	5:30	5:00	5:00	4:00	2:00
34:00	6:00	6:00	5:30	5:00	5:00	4:30	2:00
34:30	6:00	6:00	5:30	5:30	5:00	4:30	2:00
35:00	6:00	6:00	5:30	5:30	5:00	5:00	2:00

Source: *The Triathlete's Training Bible,* 2nd ed., by Joe Friel (Boulder, CO: VeloPress, 2004).

system (heart, blood, and lungs) endurance, it is a great time to branch out and explore alternative cardiovascular activities (discussed in detail in Chapter 8) in addition to focusing on form workouts for swim/bike/run (discussed in detail in Chapters 5, 6, and 7).

The Preparation phase should also be a time when you head back into the weight room. During this brief time period, you will focus on lifting light weights with high repetitions (Anatomical Adaptation or AA), which will prepare your muscles and tendons for heavier loads in the upcoming periods. You should also complete several sessions of core work each week. (Chapter 9 will discuss the off-season strength program in greater detail.)

2.4 BORG RATING OF PERCEIVED EXERTION (RPE) SCALE

ZONE		RPE	DESCRIPTION
1	Recovery	6	
1	Recovery	7	Very, very light
1	Recovery	8	
2	Extensive endurance	9	Very light
2	Extensive endurance	10	
2	Extensive endurance	11	Fairly light
3	Intensive endurance	12	
3	Intensive endurance	13	Somewhat hard
3	Intensive endurance	14	
4	Threshold	15	Hard
5a	Threshold	16	
5b	Anaerobic endurance	17	Very hard
5b	Anaerobic endurance	18	
5c	Power	19	Very, very hard
5c	Power	20	Maximal

Source: *The Triathlete's Training Bible,* 2nd ed., by Joe Friel (Boulder, CO: VeloPress, 2004).

TRAINING INTENSITY ZONES

Zone 1 (Recovery) is utilized to build early fitness and for recovery workouts. It can also be used during the recovery period during interval workouts. It is a very easy effort that you should feel you could sustain for extended periods of time.

Zone 2 (Extensive Endurance) is utilized for long endurance workouts to build a solid base and to maintain your current fitness level. As with Zone 1, you should be able to comfortably carry out a conversation in this zone for extended periods of time.

Zone 3 (Intensive Endurance) is used for early season (Base II) muscular endurance sessions.

Zones 4 and 5a (Threshold) efforts will bring you just below (Zone 4) or a bit above (Zone 5a) lactate threshold (LT) and should be used during interval sessions (work-to-rest ratio of 4:1), force work, and tempo work.

Zone 5b (Anaerobic Endurance) work is used during shorter intervals, hill, and tempo work and will require extended recovery due to the anaerobic nature of the effort. The work-to-rest ratio for intervals in this zone should follow a 1:1 pattern.

Zone 5c (Power) occurs during very fast, powerful efforts (short sprints, short steep hills) and is not often utilized by the multisport athlete. These quick, explosive intervals require a work-to-rest ratio of approximately 1:2 and require several days of recovery following the effort.

It is important for you to schedule some baseline testing in the first and last week of your Preparation phase. There are many different procedures to determine your heart rate training zones, and the ones listed in this book are simple field time trials that can be performed with minimal equipment. One piece of equipment that you *will* need to carry out the field tests is a heart rate monitor with an average heart rate function. However, if you do not have a heart rate monitor, you can use the rating of perceived exertion (RPE) to estimate your training zones until you have the appropriate equipment to complete the prescribed tests. The testing protocol for each discipline is found in Appendix D, and once you have determined your estimated lactate threshold (LT), go to Tables 2.5 and 2.6 at the end of this chapter to set your training zones.

It is possible to estimate your bike LT from your run LT and vice versa. Generally there is a 10-beat (plus or minus several beats) difference between the run (higher) and the bike (lower). So if after testing you determined that your run LT is 175, then it would be safe to say that your bike LT would be about 165. Remember that this is just an estimate, and if you find that your RPE does not match the determined training zones, you should perform a separate test in each discipline to more accurately set your training zones.

Here is a sample **Preparation training week (#2)** for an athlete who has 500 annual hours to train (please see page 169 for the workout codes). All time is expressed in hours or portions of hours.

	MON	TUE	WED	THU	FRI	SAT	SUN
Swim	0.75 S		0.75 S				
Bike				0.5 S			
Run		0.5 S					0.75 E
WTS	0.75 AA		0.75 AA		0.75 AA		
Core		0.25		0.25		0.25	
XT					RE 0.5 E	MB 1.75 E	
Time	1.5	0.75	1.5	0.75	1.25	2.0	0.75

Points to Remember for Prep

- Keep all efforts fairly easy (Zones 1–2, RPE of 6–11, or "conversational pace"—an exertion level at which you can easily carry on conversation).
- Perform testing to determine your heart rate training zones during the first week and last week in each discipline.
- Incorporate drill/form sessions into the warm-ups of your workout sessions in each discipline.
- Include stand-alone drill/form sessions in each discipline each week.

- Strength train at least two times per week; three is optimal during this phase.
- Include several core sessions each week.

BASE I

Following the Preparation phase, you will move into the base phases, starting with Base I. The Base I phase is very similar to the Preparation phase, except that the work volume slowly begins to increase. So, as with the Preparation phase, place an *X* under the Endurance and Speed abilities column on your Off-Season Training Plan Worksheet. Maintain the same training zones, keeping all your workouts at conversational pace.

You may be tempted to pick up the pace a bit, but be patient and focus on building a solid aerobic foundation. The season is a long one and there will be plenty of time for more intense sessions. Working out too hard too early in your season can head you toward early season burnout, becoming overtrained, or worse—injury.

In Base I, you will switch gears and change into a different strength-training phase (Max Transition or MT), working on developing increased strength. (See Chapter 9 for more information on strength training.) Continue to focus on form during all your other workouts, incorporating

Here is a sample **Base I training week (#1)** for an athlete who has 500 annual hours to train.

	MON	TUE	WED	THU	FRI	SAT	SUN
Swim	0.75 S		0.5 S		0.75E		
Bike		0.5 S	0.75 FG			1.5 E	
Run		0.75 S		0.5 S			1.0 E
WTS	0.75 MT			0.75 MT			
Core		0.25		0.25		0.25	
XT							MB 1.0 E
Time	1.5	1.5	1.25	1.5	.0.75	1.75	2.0

drill work into your warm-ups and completing stand-alone form sessions. Cardiovascular work can still be accomplished with alternatives to the swim/bike/run, which is especially important if you
live where the weather is inclement. (See Chapter 8 for a detailed
discussion of these alternatives.) You will also need to begin shifting
your focus to build more sport-specific endurance by increasing the
duration of your swimming, cycling, and running sessions.

Points to Remember for Base I

- Keep all efforts fairly easy (Zones 1–2, RPE of 6–11, or
  conversational pace).
- Gradually begin to increase your longest workout in each
  discipline.
- Increase your swimming, biking, and running frequency.
- Incorporate drill/form sessions into the warm-ups of your
  workout sessions in each discipline.
- Include stand-alone drill/form sessions in each discipline
  each week.
- Now that the weights are getting heavier, be sure to practice
  perfect form during your lifts.
- Continue to include several core sessions each week.

BASE II

Force and muscular endurance workouts are introduced during this
phase. So be sure to record the results of your work on improving
those abilities on your Off-Season Training Plan Worksheet, in addition to recording endurance and speed results during your "on"
weeks. The only abilities that should be marked in your "off" week are
endurance and speed. During this phase you will continue to focus on
developing your aerobic engine (continue to increase the duration of
these workouts) while introducing more force sessions, carrying over
the strength gained in the weight room from Base I during specific
swim/bike/run workouts. As you build strength in each discipline,
you are laying a strong, solid foundation upon which to build speed
later in your season—you cannot have speed without strength!

Your muscular endurance workouts should be completed at moderate intensities (Zone 3, RPE 12–14), and the force workouts should

top off at Zone 4, RPE 15. Continue to focus on your form in all disciplines and schedule heart rate zone testing during the first week of this phase. You should be well rested for your tests following the last "off" week of the Base I phase. Make sure to record your testing data after you complete each test, and adjust your zones if necessary. You will also be switching to a new phase of strength training—Power Endurance or PE. (This will be discussed in more detail in Chapter 9.)

Here is a sample **Base II training week (#3)** for an athlete who has 500 annual hours to train.

	MON	TUE	WED	THU	FRI	SAT	SUN
Swim	1.0 E		0.75 S		1.0 ME		
Bike		1.5 ME			1.0 S	2.5 E	
Run			0.5 S	0.75 F			1.5 E
WTS	1.0 SM						
Core	0.25			0.25			
XT		ET 1.0 R					MB 1.0 E
Time	2.25	2.5	1.25	1.0	2.0	2.5	2.5

Points to Remember for Base II

- Complete heart rate testing during the first week of the phase.
- Introduce force and muscular endurance workouts.
- Muscular Endurance (ME) workouts should be completed in Zone 3.
- Force workouts should top off at Zone 4.
- Continue to increase the duration of your endurance workouts.
- Incorporate drill/form sessions into the warm-ups of your workout sessions in each discipline.
- Include stand-alone drill/form sessions in each discipline each week.
- Continue to include several core sessions each week.
- Alternative cardiovascular activities can still be used but are now best reserved for easy recovery workouts.

BASE III

The final phase of your off-season is Base III, which, upon completion, should lead you into your specific build periods with a solid aerobic foundation, greater sport-specific strength, improved technique in all three disciplines, reduced limiters, and an eagerness to tackle the upcoming race season. During this phase you continue to work on all the abilities, endurance, force, speed, and muscular endurance. Your training volume will reach its maximum level during the third week of this phase, which allows you to focus more time on endurance and force workouts. As you begin more sport-specific work, decrease your strength training to one time per week, moving into the strength-maintenance phase. However, continue with your core sessions, completing at least two sessions each week—three would be optimal. Make sure to schedule your testing during the first week of Base III and record your data and adjust your zones if necessary.

Here is an example of a **Base III training week (#1)** for an athlete who has 500 annual hours to train.

	MON	TUE	WED	THU	FRI	SAT	SUN
Swim	0.75 T		1.0 E		1.0 F		
Bike	0.5 S	1.0 R		0.75 R		2.0 E	
Run		0.75 T		0.5 R	0.75 S		1.25 F
WTS						1.0 SM	
Core			0.25			0.25	
XT							
Time	1.5	1.75	1.25	1.25	1.75	3.0	1.5

Points to Remember for Base III

- Complete heart rate testing during the first week of the phase.
- Continue to focus on all of the performance abilities—endurance, force, speed, and muscular endurance.
- Continue to increase your volume gradually.
- Include more force and endurance workouts.

- Back your strength training down to 1 day per week.
- Complete at least two core sessions each week.

This chapter guided you through the specific steps of setting up a productive off-season schedule. Let's quickly review what you have accomplished in this chapter. You have:

- Determined appropriate goals and written them down.
- Identified your strengths, weaknesses, and limiters.
- Set your training objectives to address your weaknesses and limiters.
- Determined available and appropriate number of weekly hours to train and have mapped out your hours per week.
- Scheduled your Preparation, Base I, II, and III phases.
- Highlighted what abilities you will focus on in each phase.
- Set your heart rate training zones for cycling and running and determined your 100 yard/meter pace for the swim.

The remaining chapters of this book will address the important components that you will need to focus on to have a productive and enjoyable off-season. The information that you will gain from these chapters will aid you in developing your daily workouts within each of the phases of the off-season. Each chapter will feature sample workouts that you can use as examples for designing workouts that fit your individual needs. Be thoughtful in your planning, consistent with your training, creative with your workouts, and you will find yourself fully charged and eager for your upcoming season.

REFERENCES

Bernhardt, Gale. *Training Plans for Multisport Athletes.* Boulder, CO: VeloPress, 2000.

Bompa, Tudor. *Periodization, Theory, and Methodology of Training.* Champaign, IL: Human Kinetics, 1999.

Friel, Joe. *The Triathlete's Training Bible.* 2nd ed. Boulder, CO: VeloPress, 2004.

Jansen, Peter. *Training Lactate Pulse-Rate.* Oulu, Finland: Polar Electro Oy, 1992.

Weinberg, Robert, and Daniel Gould. *Foundations of Sport and Exercise Psychology.* 3rd ed. Champaign, IL: Human Kinetics, 2003.

2.5 CYCLING HEART RATE ZONES

Find your lactate threshold (LT) heart rate (bold) in the "Zone 5a" column. Then read across left and right for training zones.

ZONE 1 RECOVERY	ZONE 2 EXTENSIVE ENDURANCE	ZONE 3 INTENSIVE ENDURANCE	ZONE 4 SUB-THRESHOLD	ZONE 5A SUPER-THRESHOLD	ZONE 5B ANAEROBIC ENDURANCE	ZONE 5C POWER
90–108	109–122	123–128	129–136	**137–140**	141–145	146–150
91–109	110–123	124–129	130–137	**138–141**	142–146	147–151
91–109	110–124	125–130	131–138	**139–142**	143–147	148–152
92–110	111–125	126–130	131–139	**140–143**	144–147	148–153
92–111	112–125	126–131	132–140	**141–144**	145–148	149–154
93–112	113–126	127–132	133–141	**142–145**	146–149	150–155
94–112	113–127	128–133	134–142	**143–145**	146–150	151–156
94–113	114–128	129–134	135–143	**144–147**	148–151	152–157
95–114	115–129	130–135	136–144	**145–148**	149–152	153–158
95–115	116–130	131–136	137–145	**146–149**	150–154	155–159
97–116	117–131	132–137	138–146	**147–150**	151–155	156–161
97–117	118–132	133–138	139–147	**148–151**	152–156	157–162
98–118	119–133	134–139	140–148	**149–152**	153–157	158–163
98–119	120–134	135–140	141–149	**150–153**	154–158	159–164
99–120	121–134	135–141	142–150	**151–154**	155–159	160–165
100–121	122–135	136–142	143–151	**152–155**	156–160	161–166
100–122	123–136	137–142	143–152	**153–156**	157–161	162–167
101–123	124–137	138–143	144–153	**154–157**	158–162	163–168
101–124	125–138	139–144	145–154	**155–158**	159–163	164–169
102–125	126–138	139–145	146–155	**156–159**	160–164	165–170
103–126	127–140	141–146	147–156	**157–160**	161–165	166–171
104–127	128–141	142–147	148–157	**158–161**	162–167	168–173
104–128	129–142	143–148	149–158	**159–162**	163–168	169–174
105–129	130–143	144–148	149–159	**160–163**	164–169	170–175
106–129	130–143	144–150	151–160	**161–164**	165–170	171–176
106–130	131–144	145–151	152–161	**162–165**	166–171	172–177
107–131	132–145	146–152	153–162	**163–166**	167–172	173–178
107–132	133–146	147–153	154–163	**164–167**	168–173	174–179
108–133	134–147	148–154	155–164	**165–168**	169–174	175–180

2.5 (CONTINUED) CYCLING HEART RATE ZONES

Find your lactate threshold (LT) heart rate (bold) in the "Zone 5a" column. Then read across left and right for training zones.

ZONE 1 RECOVERY	ZONE 2 EXTENSIVE ENDURANCE	ZONE 3 INTENSIVE ENDURANCE	ZONE 4 SUB-THRESHOLD	ZONE 5A SUPER-THRESHOLD	ZONE 5B ANAEROBIC ENDURANCE	ZONE 5C POWER
109–134	135–148	149–154	155–165	**166–169**	170–175	176–181
109–135	136–149	150–155	156–166	**167–170**	171–176	177–182
110–136	137–150	151–156	157–167	**168–171**	172–177	178–183
111–137	138–151	152–157	158–168	**169–172**	173–178	179–185
112–138	139–151	152–158	159–169	**170–173**	174–179	180–186
112–139	140–152	153–160	161–170	**171–174**	175–180	181–187
113–140	141–153	154–160	161–171	**172–175**	176–181	182–188
113–141	142–154	155–161	162–172	**173–176**	177–182	183–189
114–142	143–155	156–162	163–173	**174–177**	178–183	184–190
115–143	144–156	157–163	164–174	**175–178**	179–184	185–191
115–144	145–157	158–164	165–175	**176–179**	180–185	186–192
116–145	146–158	159–165	166–176	**177–180**	181–186	187–193
116–146	147–159	160–166	167–177	**178–181**	182–187	188–194
117–147	148–160	161–166	167–178	**179–182**	183–188	189–195
118–148	149–160	161–167	168–179	**180–183**	184–190	191–197
119–149	150–161	162–168	169–180	**181–184**	185–191	192–198
119–150	151–162	163–170	171–181	**182–185**	186–192	193–199
120–151	152–163	164–171	172–182	**183–186**	187–193	194–200
121–152	153–164	165–172	173–183	**184–187**	188–194	195–201
121–153	154–165	166–172	173–184	**185–188**	189–195	196–202
122–154	155–166	167–173	174–185	**186–189**	190–196	197–203
122–155	156–167	168–174	175–186	**187–190**	191–197	198–204
123–156	157–168	169–175	176–187	**188–191**	192–198	199–205
124–157	158–169	170–176	177–188	**189–192**	193–199	200–206
124–158	159–170	171–177	178–189	**190–193**	194–200	201–207
125–159	160–170	171–178	179–190	**191–194**	195–201	202–208
125–160	161–171	172–178	179–191	**192–195**	196–202	203–209
126–161	162–172	173–179	180–192	**193–196**	197–203	204–210
127–162	163–173	174–180	181–193	**194–197**	198–204	205–211
127–163	164–174	175–181	182–194	**195–198**	199–205	206–212

Source: *The Triathlete's Training Bible,* 2nd ed., by Joe Friel (Boulder, CO: VeloPress, 2004).

2.6 RUNNING HEART RATE ZONES

Find your lactate threshold (LT) heart rate (bold) in the "Zone 5a" column. Then read across left and right for training zones.

ZONE 1 RECOVERY	ZONE 2 EXTENSIVE ENDURANCE	ZONE 3 INTENSIVE ENDURANCE	ZONE 4 SUB–THRESHOLD	ZONE 5A SUPER–THRESHOLD	ZONE 5B ANAEROBIC ENDURANCE	ZONE 5C POWER
93–119	120–126	127–133	134–139	**140–143**	144–149	150–156
94–119	120–127	128–134	135–140	**141–144**	145–150	151–157
95–120	121–129	130–135	136–141	**142–145**	146–151	152–158
95–121	122–130	131–136	137–142	**143–146**	147–152	153–159
96–122	123–131	132–137	138–143	**144–147**	148–153	154–160
96–123	124–132	133–138	139–144	**145–148**	149–154	155–161
97–124	125–133	134–139	140–145	**146–149**	150–155	156–162
97–124	125–134	135–140	141–146	**147–150**	151–156	157–163
98–125	126–135	136–141	142–147	**148–151**	152–157	158–164
99–126	127–135	136–142	143–148	**149–152**	153–158	159–165
99–127	128–136	137–143	144–149	**150–153**	154–158	159–166
100–128	129–137	138–144	144–150	**151–154**	155–159	160–167
100–129	130–138	139–145	146–151	**152–155**	156–160	161–168
101–130	131–139	140–146	147–152	**153–156**	157–161	162–169
102–131	132–140	141–147	148–153	**154–157**	158–162	163–170
103–131	132–141	142–148	149–154	**155–158**	158–164	165–172
103–132	133–142	143–149	150–155	**156–159**	160–165	166–173
104–133	134–143	144–150	151–156	**157–160**	161–166	167–174
105–134	135–143	144–151	152–157	**158–161**	162–167	168–175
105–135	136–144	145–152	153–158	**159–162**	163–168	169–176
106–136	137–145	146–153	154–159	**160–163**	164–169	170–177
106–136	137–146	147–154	155–160	**161–164**	165–170	171–178
107–137	138–147	148–155	156–161	**162–165**	166–171	172–179
108–138	139–148	149–155	156–162	**163–166**	167–172	173–180
109–139	140–149	150–156	157–163	**164–167**	168–174	175–182
109–140	141–150	151–157	158–164	**165–168**	169–175	176–183
110–141	142–151	152–158	159–165	**166–169**	170–176	177–184
111–141	142–152	153–159	160–166	**167–170**	171–177	178–185
111–142	143–153	154–160	161–167	**168–171**	172–178	179–186
111–143	144–154	155–161	162–168	**169–172**	173–179	180–187

2.6 (CONTINUED) RUNNING HEART RATE ZONES

Find your lactate threshold (LT) heart rate (bold) in the "Zone 5a" column. Then read across left and right for training zones.

ZONE 1 RECOVERY	ZONE 2 EXTENSIVE ENDURANCE	ZONE 3 INTENSIVE ENDURANCE	ZONE 4 SUB- THRESHOLD	ZONE 5A SUPER- THRESHOLD	ZONE 5B ANAEROBIC ENDURANCE	ZONE 5C POWER
112–144	145–155	156–162	163–169	**170–173**	174–179	180–188
113–145	146–156	157–163	164–170	**171–174**	175–180	181–189
114–145	146–156	157–164	165–171	**172–175**	176–182	183–191
115–146	147–157	158–165	166–172	**173–176**	177–183	184–192
115–147	148–157	158–166	167–173	**174–177**	178–184	185–193
116–148	149–158	159–167	168–174	**175–178**	179–185	186–194
117–149	150–159	160–168	169–175	**176–179**	180–186	187–195
117–150	151–160	161–169	170–176	**177–180**	181–187	188–196
118–151	152–161	162–170	171–177	**178–181**	182–188	189–197
118–152	153–162	163–171	172–178	**179–182**	183–189	190–198
119–153	164–163	164–172	173–179	**180–183**	184–190	191–199
120–154	155–164	165–173	174–180	**181–184**	185–192	193–201
121–154	155–165	166–174	175–181	**182–185**	186–193	194–202
121–155	156–166	167–175	176–182	**183–186**	187–194	195–203
122–156	157–167	168–176	177–183	**184–187**	188–195	196–204
123–157	158–168	169–177	178–184	**185–188**	189–196	197–205
123–158	159–169	170–178	179–185	**186–189**	190–197	198–206
124–159	160–170	171–179	180–186	**187–190**	191–198	199–207
125–160	161–171	172–180	181–188	**189–192**	193–200	201–209
126–161	162–172	173–181	182–189	**190–193**	194–201	202–210
126–162	163–173	174–182	183–190	**191–194**	195–201	202–211
127–163	164–174	175–183	184–191	**192–195**	196–202	203–212
127–164	165–175	176–184	185–192	**193–196**	197–203	204–213
128–165	166–176	177–185	186–193	**194–197**	198–294	205–214
129–165	166–177	178–186	187–194	**195–198**	199–205	206–215
129–166	167–178	179–187	188–195	**196–199**	200–206	207–216
130–167	168–178	179–188	189–196	**197–198**	199–207	208–217
130–168	169–179	180–189	190–197	**198–201**	202–208	209–218
131–169	170–180	181–190	191–198	**199–202**	203–209	210–219
132–170	171–181	182–191	192–199	**200–203**	204–210	211–220

Source: *The Triathlete's Training Bible*, 2nd ed. by Joe Friel (Boulder, CO: VeloPress, 2004).

3 Core Strength:

UTILIZING THE SWISS AND MEDICINE BALLS

Most people are familiar with the saying, "A chain is only as strong as its weakest link," and such can be said about the core strength of an athlete (i.e., muscles of the abdominal area and back, sometimes called the torso). A strong core creates the major "link" in the body's musculoskeletal chain. *A strong core forms the foundation for solid fitness and athletic performance.* The core is the athlete's center of power, providing support during swimming, biking, and running. Targeting this area for development can only improve athletic performance.

Developing a strong core is more than just showcasing the traditional "six-pack abs." A strong center of power translates into total body power, speed, quickness, effectiveness, efficiency, coordination, and agility. All lower and upper body movements are *originated from, stabilized by, transferred through* the core.

CORE FACTS

- The trunk and lower torso equal over 50 percent of the body's total mass.
- The muscles of the core are responsible for maintaining the body's equilibrium during exercise.
- The core muscles assist in breathing.

- The abdominal and back muscles protect the body's vital organs, nervous system, and spinal cord.
- The core muscles are the link for efficient and proper movement during exercise.
- The abdominal muscles help to support the spine, allowing you to stand erect, and also help to reduce lower back stress.

A properly developed core helps an athlete move more efficiently during running, swimming, and biking. Let's take a more in-depth look at the benefits of a solid core in each of the three triathlon disciplines.

CORE STRENGTH BENEFITS FOR THE RUNNER

Because running is a linear activity, all movement should be straight ahead. Any side-to-side swinging of the arms, torso, or legs wastes energy, and these extraneous movements can cost an athlete time. A strong core will keep the body erect, "running tall," while keeping the breathing pathways unrestricted. A runner who is "running tall" has proper posture/body alignment. Since force during movement is transferred most efficiently in a straight line, proper body alignment is critical. A poorly developed core can cause poor posture, breaking that straight line or link. A supportive core will help you conserve energy by linking a strong, "quiet," upper body that is moving forward with the power of the lower limbs in motion, making every stride more effective. A more effective stride leads to greater efficiency for longer periods of time. A weak core that leads to poor posture or body alignment can also place stress on joints, muscles, and tendons, often leading to injury.

CORE STRENGTH BENEFITS FOR THE CYCLIST

Proper posture on the bike is the foundation for sound technique. The core becomes the link between the power put out by the lower body to turn the cranks and the strength of the upper body, which braces against the handlebars, absorbing the shock of the road. A weak core can disrupt this flow of force, causing unnecessary body movements, which in turn waste energy and make the rider less aerodynamic. Thus, a strong core aids in a rider's overall efficiency on the bike. A strong core can also prevent the lower-back fatigue and pain that far too often plague triathletes.

In all positions on the bike—whether your hands are on the drops, hoods, or aerobars, or you are seated or standing—your back will be in a somewhat flexed position. The longer the duration of the ride, the longer these muscles are taxed and the greater the chance for a break-down in form or injury. Strengthening the muscles of the back, from the lower back to the base of the skull, will help reduce fatigue and discomfort of the lower back, as well as allow the rider to transfer power more efficiently and to remain in the aero position for extended periods of time.

CORE STRENGTH BENEFITS FOR THE SWIMMER

Of the three triathlon disciplines, swimming is the most technical, and it has the added dimension of being performed in a resistive (aqueous) environment. Proper body posture/alignment is important for efficient movement through the water; and core strength, once again, is the stabilizing factor. The resistance of the water, especially coupled with an athlete's poor alignment, can cause additional drag on the swimmer, leading to decreased efficiency. This in turn will slow down the swimmer and may well cause increased fatigue in longer swims.

To move through the water in the most efficient manner, you must be "streamlined," maintaining an imaginary straight line running from the top of your head, through the midline, on down to the feet. This streamlined position, supported by a strong core, ensures that you use all of your energy to move forward in the water, rather than wasting energy through vertical or side-to-side movements.

In swimming, as in running and cycling, your strong core becomes the link between the power generated by the upper and the lower body. As the streamlined swimmer "rolls" from his left side to his right side, much of the power from the stroke is generated by his core. Any weakness in the core can lead to improper technique, subsequent fatigue, and added stress to the shoulders. Consequently, a weak core can be one of the factors that contributes to shoulder instability and pain, often leading to "swimmer's shoulder." To summarize, a solid core will provide the swimmer with correct posture/alignment and balance in the water, which will minimize drag, increase efficiency, reduce the likelihood of injury, and improve one's effective movement through the water.

EXERCISES TO DEVELOP A STRONG CORE

The exercises listed in this section will target the core area—hip, back, and abdominal muscles. These exercises can be done at the gym or at home with minimal equipment. All exercises below can be done by time—three sets (more or less) of 20 seconds (more or less) or by number—three sets (more or less) of ten repetitions (more or less). As with any new exercise in your workout regime, make sure that you build duration and repetition frequency gradually, and increase the resistance slowly. Also, make sure that you are fully recovered from one session before completing another session (allow at least one day between the core sessions). If at any time you experience discomfort or pain, especially in your back, do not continue. Mix and match these exercises, balancing back and abdominal exercises, and turn your core into your strongest link.

Equipment Needed

Medicine Ball (6–8 pounds)
Swiss Ball

Body Weight Exercises

Basic Crunch

Lie flat on the ground with your knees bent in a traditional sit-up position. Cross your arms on your chest or place your hands over your ears. Focus your eyes on the ceiling to avoid putting stress on your neck. Slowly lift your shoulder blades off the floor, crunch your abdominal muscles, hold, and lower. Complete each movement as a separate step.

3.1

Twisting Crunch

3.2

Lie flat on the ground with your knees bent in a traditional sit-up position. Cross your arms on your chest or place your hands over your ears. Focus your eyes on the ceiling to avoid putting stress on your neck. Slowly lift your shoulder blades off the floor, crunch your abdominals, and twist to the right, hold, back to center, and lower. Repeat the same movements, this time twisting to the left side. Complete each movement as a separate step.

Pike

3.3

Place your body in the up-phase of the push-up position with your hips slightly higher than normal. Keep your elbows about 6 inches apart, placing them directly under your shoulders with elbows, forearms, and hands on the ground, palms together. Keep your shoulder blades flat and your back straight. Your legs should be extended straight and balanced on your toes. Hold this position for 15 seconds: Move your elbows forward 2 inches, and hold for 15 seconds. Once more, move your elbows forward another 2 inches, and hold again for 15 seconds. Rest for 30 seconds and repeat.

Superman

Lie face down with your arms and legs extended straight ahead and behind. Your head should be in line with your spine. Lift your left arm, hand out as in a handshake, and your right leg, initiating the movement with your glutes (butt muscles), and hold for 10 seconds. Release and repeat with your right arm and left leg. Alternate each side for a series for each set.

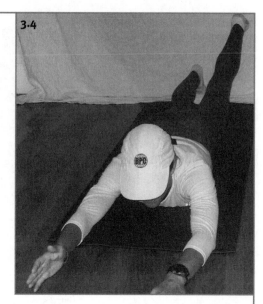

3.4

Superman Variations
- Single-arm raise
- Double-arm raise
- Single-leg raise
- Double-leg raise
- Opposite leg/arm extension
- Same side leg/arm extension

These variations can also be completed using a Swiss ball.

Keeping your hands and feet in contact with the floor, lie on the ball stomach-down (the ball should be centered at your midsection). Attempt various superman movements.

Medicine Ball Exercises

Mini Crunch

Begin in the basic crunch position (knees bent), starting with the ball under your head (as if on a pillow) and your hands on either side  of the ball. The movement involves small crunches, using your abdominals to lift your trunk, head, and ball just off the floor, concentrating on contracting the abs. Repeat the movement for 30 to 60 seconds.

Toe Touch

Begin by lying flat on your back (legs out straight), with your arms extended behind your head, holding the medicine ball. Same explosive movement as in the mini crunch, except that the ball is "thrown" to the ankles. Repeat the movement for 30 to 60 seconds.

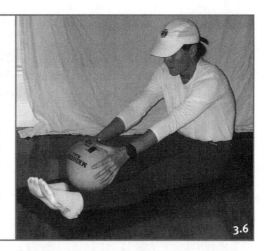

The Hinge

Begin in a seated position on the end of a chair or bench. Hold the medicine ball between your knees, with your hands behind your body holding the sides of the chair or bench for stability. Crunch your knees to your chest and release. Repeat the movement for 30 to 60 seconds.

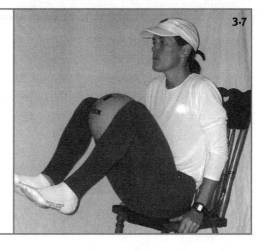

Soccer Throw

Begin in the basic crunch position (knees bent), starting with arms extended behind the head, on the floor, holding the medicine ball. The movement is explosive, bringing the ball from behind the head and "throwing" it as the body is brought forward into a full sit-up position (the ball is "thrown" into the lap). Repeat movement for 30 to 60 seconds.

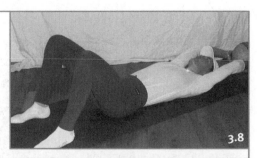

Swiss Ball Exercises

Rollout

Kneel in front of the ball. Tighten your glutes and draw your navel in (pelvic tilt). Place your hands on the top of the ball and raise your feet off the ground (knees become the pivot

point). Walk your hands out on the ball—both of your arms and the ball will move away from your body. Once you feel your abdominals engage, you are at the starting position. Your hands are stationary. Pivot on your knees, moving your torso and hips forward as the ball rolls away from your knees. Try to keep your chest upright and do not hyperextend your back—keep a straight line through your upper body. Hold that extended position for 2 seconds, roll back, and repeat.

Crunch

Sit on the ball and roll your hips forward until they just move off of the ball. As you walk your feet out away from the ball, your upper body becomes more horizontal and your lower back should be supported by the curve of the ball. Place hands at your ears or cross your arms over your chest. "Crunch" forward slowly, as in the beginning of a sit-up, until your abdominals are

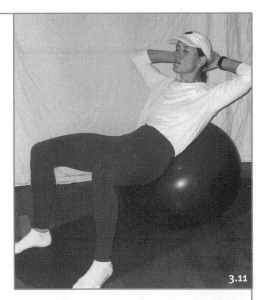

3.11

fully engaged (sitting up too far engages your hip flexors and negates the value for your abs). Keep a neutral neck position. Slowly lower your upper body to the starting position, focusing on your abdominal muscles, and repeat.

3.12

Side Crunch

Place the ball 3 to 4 feet from a wall. Then lean on the ball sideways so that your hips are just below the top of the ball and your feet are braced against the wall. (Use your feet to stabilize your body so that you do not roll forward.) Place your hands at your ears. Slowly crunch up until your knees, hips, and shoulders are aligned; then return to the starting position and repeat.

CORE RESOURCES

www.power-systems.com and **www.performbetter.com—**
These Web sites offer mail order for Swiss balls, medicine balls, and
other training products.

REFERENCES

Alfieri, RoseMarie Gionta. *Functional Training: Everyone's Guide to the New Fitness Revolution.* Long Island City, NY: Hatherleigh Press, 2001.

Brittenham, Dean, and Greg Brittenham. *Stronger Abs and Back: 165 Exercises to Build Your Center of Power.* Champaign, IL: Human Kinetics, 1997.

Burke, Edmund R., ed. *High-Tech Cycling: The Science of Riding Faster.* 2nd ed. Champaign, IL: Human Kinetics, 2003.

Davis, Phinney, and Connie Carpenter. *Training for Cycling: The Ultimate Guide to Improved Performance.* New York: Penguin Publishing, Perigee Books, 1992.

Goldenberg, Lorne, and Peter Twist. *Strength Ball Training.* Champaign, IL: Human Kinetics, 2002.

CHAPTER

4 Flexibility:

YOGA FOR MULTISPORT ATHLETES

Yoga is a centuries-old Eastern philosophy that is practiced by people in all walks of life, all over the world. The term "yoga" translates into "yoke" or "union," describing the process of achieving balance between mind and body. Initially, the sole purpose of yoga was to experience spiritual enlightenment through the practice of various meditative and physical exercises. As the practice has evolved over time and a variety of yoga disciplines have developed, more and more athletes are becoming yoga proponents. Practicing yoga on a regular basis builds more than a strong, flexible body. It promotes balance and relaxation, increases range of motion, stresses the importance of coordinating breathing with movement, and strengthens intrinsic muscle groups that stabilize the skeletal system.

Yoga can be a wonderful addition to any training regimen, and with its current popularity it will not be difficult to find class offerings in your area. To find a yoga class you can check the yellow pages or classified ads in your local paper, inquire at health clubs or your local YMCA, or, best of all, ask friends, associates, or training partners for referrals.

The majority of the classes in the United States teach one of the many varieties of hatha yoga, a physical discipline that focuses on asanas (postures) and breath work. Before you choose a yoga class to attend, make sure that you look into the instructor's background and learn what form of yoga he or she teaches. (Some approaches are quite vigorous, while others are more gentle.) You will want to be sure to find a beginner's class, regardless of how outstanding you feel you are as an athlete. It's also very important for you to let your instructor know of any physical problems or limitations you have so that he or she can help you adapt yogic positions. Additionally, some instructors offer special classes for people with a history of back injuries or other such issues.

If you have challenges either finding a class in your area or finding classes that fit your schedule, you can also choose from the many yoga instruction videos on the market, or you may find classes that you can follow on television. Once you have narrowed your search, you will want to answer such questions as: How much does the class cost? How long is the class and how many people are enrolled? (A class that is too big can limit the personal attention you receive.) What kind of clothing is recommended? Does the class provide a yoga mat, or do you need to purchase one?

So, if you aren't already practicing yoga, try something new this off-season and you, too, can be on your way to becoming a more balanced, relaxed, focused, and effective athlete.

GETTING THE MOST FROM YOUR YOGA CLASS

The following are some tips to help you maximize the benefits of your yoga class. As with any exercises, the better prepared you are, the clearer you are about your purpose. And the more you dedicate yourself to continuity (i.e., regular attendance and practice), the better your results will be.

- Try to get to the class about 10 minutes early to roll out your mat and to get focused for the session.
- As with other exercise sessions, try not to eat right before the class (eat at least 2 hours prior to the class).
- Attend the class as often as possible (this gives the instructor time to know you so that he or she can tailor postures to suit your needs).
- Do not perform any postures that cause pain, especially in the knees, lower back, and neck.
- Let the instructor know if you have an injury or condition that might prevent certain postures.

- Let the instructor know that a certain posture causes pain and then ask for an alternative posture, or stop and rest until the next posture is presented.
- It is common for instructors to aid students with various postures. Make sure that you are comfortable with the contact, and, if the "help" is causing any pain, let the instructor know immediately.
- Concentrate on the task at hand (not the list of things that you need to get done, or whom you need to call, or how badly your last meeting went).
- Leave your cell phone and pager behind.
- If attending with a friend, keep the conversation down as you may distract others.
- If you sweat a lot, make sure that you have a towel and bring your own mat.
- Bring a water bottle to class.
- Work at your own pace (all bodies are not created equal).
- Try not to enter late or leave class early, as it can be disruptive to others.

YOGA BREATHING EXERCISE

Often during competition, especially in long-distance events, you can lose your focus, your confidence level can drop, and/or you can start to doubt yourself and have negative thoughts. You can either let this negative energy drag you down, or you can change your focus to recharge yourself and continue on. An essential technique practiced in yoga is focused breathing.

If you begin to lose your focus in a competition and your performance starts to suffer, take a deep, slow inhalation and imagine that with each breath you "recharge" your energy. With each exhalation, focus on releasing the tension in your face, neck, shoulders, trunk, arms, and legs. Feel the tension flow out of your body from top to bottom as you decrease your negative thoughts.

This is a simple technique that can be practiced while working at your desk or driving your car. Try it a few times and feel the tension melt away. The next time you take that negative dip out on the racecourse, you will have another effective technique in your arsenal to get you back on track.

SUGGESTED SIMPLE YOGA POSTURES FOR TRIATHLETES

Salutation to the Sun (a Series of Poses)

Mountain

Stand straight with your feet together, shoulders back, hands at your side. Move your hands together into a "prayer" position, arms bent at the elbow (see Photo 4.1). While inhaling smoothly and deeply, stretch up, raising your arms over your head, and gradually lean back (see Photo 4.2). Hold that position briefly and then slowly fall forward into a forward bend.

Forward Bend

Bend forward (see Photo 4.3) and touch the floor with your fingertips or palms of your hands in front of your feet and pull your face close to your legs (or if you cannot touch the floor easily, instead hold onto your elbows and bend as far toward your legs as you can comfortably go as shown in Photo 4.4). Make sure that you do not lock your knees. Inhale and look up, and then exhale and move into plank position.

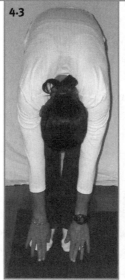

Plank Position

Bring your left foot back into a lunge position and bend your right knee (see Photo 4.5). Inhale and then bring your right foot back next to the left into a "push-up" position. Your elbows are straight and your hands should be directly under your shoulders (see Photo 4.6). Then move into the upward facing dog position.

Upward Facing Dog

Lower your body, elbows bent, palms flat. Your hands, chin, knees, and toes should be in contact with the floor, and your stomach should be slightly raised (see Photo 4.7). Exhale. Then straighten your arms while arching your back. Look up, with your head, shoulders, and chest raised, as you keep the rest of your body touching the floor (see Photo 4.8). Inhale. Then move into the downward facing dog position.

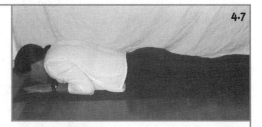

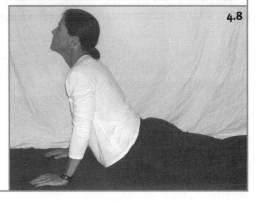

Downward Facing Dog

Raise and then bend your body to form a peak, looking at your shins while keeping your arms and legs straight (see Photo 4.9). Take five long breathes and on the next inhale bring your left foot forward between your arms into a lunge position (see Photo 4.10). Bring your right foot forward next to your left foot, straighten your legs in a relaxed way, and hang your upper torso and head, touching fingertips to the floor (see Photo 4.11). Exhale. Raise your head and torso, stretch upward, and lift your arms over your head. Look up and gradually lean back (see Photo 4.12). Inhale and return to the start position, arms bent at the elbow, hands together in a prayer position.

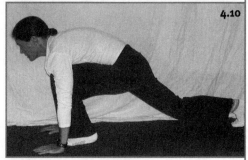

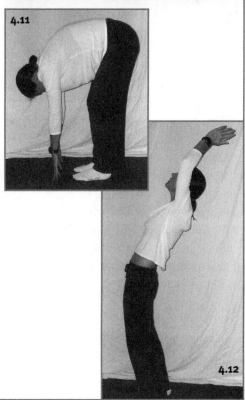

Each of these poses can be performed independently, but when combined, they are a great warm-up for you before you hop into the pool, jump on your bike, or head out for a run. Repeat the sequence several times, gradually building the pace, for a solid warm-up, or execute the sequence slowly for a relaxing and calming cool-down. The off-season is the most opportune time of year to add something new to your daily training plan. Join a yoga class or buy an instruction tape and break free from your usual routine—you will be pleased with your improved flexibility and concentration during your upcoming season.

YOGA RESOURCES

www.yogafinder.com—This site contains a nationwide state-by-state directory of yoga classes.

www.yogasite.com—This site contains a wide variety of yoga-related information and links.

REFERENCES

Birch, Beryl. *Power Yoga: The Total Strength and Flexibility Workout.* New York, NY: Fireside, 1995.

Couch, Jean. *The Runner's Yoga Book: A Balanced Approach to Fitness.* Berkeley, CA: Rodmell Press, 1990.

Kogler, Aladar. *Yoga for Athletes: Secrets of an Olympic Coach.* 4th ed. St. Paul, MN: Llewellyn Publications, 1999.

CHAPTER

5 Swimming:

DRILL TO PERFECTION

Swimming is the most technically demanding of the three triathlon disciplines, and the off-season is an ideal time to improve your swim technique. This means slowing down to focus on form to become a more efficient swimmer. You should ignore the pace clock. And if you swim with others, resist the temptation to keep up with them. Swimming fast with poor technique will just reinforce old and sometimes harmful habits. Do not worry about losing your fitness in the pool, for drill work during the off-season will help you maintain your aerobic engine while you practice perfecting your form.

Incorporate drills early in your workout session so that you are fresh when you perform them. Practicing drills while fatigued will cause you to resort to your old habits, reinforcing incorrect form. Keep the drill segments short, 25 to 50 yards, and make sure that you rest adequately before performing the next repetition. Your drill pace should be slow and purposeful (meaning focused on proper form). Once you feel competent with the particular drill, you can increase your speed a bit. If, however, you feel as though your form is breaking down, slow down. Try to focus on one aspect of your stroke during the particular drill. It is easier to focus on one area of your stroke at a time (for example, high elbow recovery) than to also worry about your head position, hand entry, rotation, etc. It is best to perform one part perfectly, then switch your focus to another part of your stroke.

For triathletes, swimming is more about consistently efficient technique than about levels of fitness or strength. Your goal in the pool is to achieve perfect form and thus to become a more efficient swimmer. In triathlon competition, a more efficient swimmer emerges from the water well warmed up and ready for the bike—not exhausted and frustrated from having wasted energy due to poor form. Efficiency and the speed it produces can only come after you have achieved a solid base of good form and developed that form into habit. Remember to make swimming drill work a priority in your off-season and you will transform your body's efficiency in the water, performing at a more balanced, smooth, effortless, and faster level.

DRILL STRATEGIES

To sum things up, here are the points you want to remember as you train in the off-season to perfect your swim form and thus improve your efficiency and speed.

- Complete drills at the beginning of your workout, while you are still fresh.
- Keep the drill repeats short.
- Rest an adequate amount of time between repetitions.
- Slow down so that you concentrate on form, not speed.
- Focus on one aspect of your stroke at a time.
- Reinforce the perfect form you achieve by repeating it until it becomes habit.

PERFECTING YOUR FREESTYLE STROKE

The following points break down the freestyle stroke into nine main components. Thinking about and working on these individually during your swim sessions will help ensure that you develop an effective and efficient stroke.

Head Position

Your head position will dictate the position of the rest of your body. Your face should be down, eyes looking slightly forward, with the water hitting at your hairline.If you totally submerge your head, it will become a source of resistance (your head weighs quite a bit!), and if you raise your head to look up, not only will your neck and upper back become fatigued, but your hips will drop, causing you to "drag" your lower body through the water.

Body Position

If your head is correctly positioned, and your neck and upper back muscles are relaxed, your body should also be correctly positioned, parallel to the bottom of the pool.

Body Rotation

With each arm stroke, your body should pivot from side to side. When your right arm is fully extended as your left arm is in the final stage of recovering, the entire right side of your body should face the bottom of the pool, while your entire left side should point upward. Your hips should initiate your body rotation: As they begin to rotate, the rest of your body will follow, remaining in a straight line.

The Reach

When you reach forward, extend your arm out completely and then stretch a bit more by extending from your shoulder. The added extension from your shoulder helps to lengthen your stroke, which will increase your efficiency.

The Pull

The pull is the power part of your stroke, and you want to "grab" as much water as possible with each stroke. Imagine you are reaching over a barrel so that the water is in contact with your entire arm. As it moves through the water, your arm should follow an S pattern. With your elbow high as you are "catching" the water, your hand should move in toward your midline and then out toward your hip as it exits the water for the finish of the stroke.

The Finish

As you are finishing your stroke past your hip, be sure to extend your arm fully so that your thumbs rub past your upper thigh. This will help you to keep your stroke long, rather than short and choppy.

The Kick

Focus on a natural rhythm for your kick and remember that for longer distance events, kicking is used more to keep your lower body riding high in the water than for propulsion.

Head Position for Breathing

Concentrate on keeping your head movement as limited as possible, turning your head up so that just one eye is above the waterline. Pretend that there is a string attached to your chin and that there is a gentle tug each time you go to take a breath. Too much head movement can cause your body to follow in-line and create a snaking motion in the water.

Breathing Pattern

Bilateral breathing (breathing on both your left and right sides) will help you even out your stroke and will keep you better balanced in the water. It also provides you with a more versatile breathing option if weather conditions (sun or choppy water) prevent you from breathing on your favored side. Make sure that when you exhale, you do so through your nose. Repeatedly getting water in your nose can cause sinus irritation and will also interrupt your stroke, causing you to slow or stop to clear your breathing passages. A slow, relaxed exhale through your nose will prevent this annoying problem.

If you have never had your stroke critiqued, the off-season is the perfect time to have this done. Try to locate a swim coach (high school or United States Swimming) or a masters program (United States Masters Swimming) in your area. Make sure that the masters program allows time for stroke instruction, improvement, and feedback and is not just a "yardage" workout.

"OTHER" STROKES

The off-season is also a great time to teach yourself the "other" strokes: butterfly (or "fly" for short), backstroke, and breaststroke. Learning these strokes will aid you in perfecting your balance and refining your form, as well as working other muscles that are not taxed while swimming freestyle. Mixing up your strokes will also help prevent injuries by giving your freestyle muscles a rest. The backstroke can help you maintain a streamlined body position and reinforce good body rotation. It also works your freestyle muscles in the opposite direction, helping to keep your shoulders loose. During an open-water swim, the backstroke can come in handy if you get into some difficulty (kicked, goggles knocked loose, trouble breathing), allowing you to flip over on your back to regain your composure. The butterfly helps you develop a strong pull, and the kick is great for developing a strong core. The breaststroke will help you develop strong inner and outer thighs, upper arms, and pectorals. It is a great stroke to utilize in an open-water swim when you need to quickly check your bearings or maneuver through a turn-around.

FLIP TURNS

Many triathletes feel there is no need to learn to complete a flip turn because they do not use it in the open water. But when training in the pool, every time you come to the wall, grab on, and switch directions, you get a bit of a break. In an hour swim session, this time adds up to a lot of rest, which would not occur if you were flip turning off the wall or in the open water. A flip turn will allow you to swim more continuously and will also help with breath control. If you think of a flip turn as just a somersault, break it down into several steps, and are patient, you can learn to do it confidently after a bit practice.

Steps to a Successful Freestyle Flip Turn

Start—As your head crosses the *T* (yes, that black line at the bottom of the pool serves a purpose as you are now about 2 feet from the wall), you should be completing your last stroke and this will initiate your somersault. Tuck your chin into your chest, dolphin kick while finishing your pull, ending with both your arms at your side. As you start this motion, begin to exhale through your nose. This will prevent water from going up into your nose and making the flip turn a very unpleasant experience.

Tuck—You should already have started your downward motion from the initial head tuck and dolphin kick. Now finish your somersault by allowing your body to follow your head, tucking into a ball (knees and feet pulled in tight). At this point you may feel like you are losing some momentum, so now is the time to use your arms to keep the somersault going. Keep your elbows at your side and use your forearms to push the water toward your head. This should help you finish the last head-over-heels phase of the flip turn and get you in the proper position to push off the wall.

Finish—As you finish the somersault, your legs are still bent at the knees (at almost a 90-degree angle) as your feet squarely hit the wall. When you hit the wall, release your elbows from the side of your body, bring your hands together, and shoot your arms straight over your head (into a streamlined position).

Land—When you first hit the wall, your face should be looking up, about a foot below the surface of the water. You will straighten your legs quickly and powerfully, and your entire body should be parallel to the bottom of the pool. If executed correctly, you will be in a perfect streamlined position, heading toward the other end of the pool.

Streamline — Push off the wall, maintaining your streamlined position. As you improve and become more confident with your flip

SWIM AIDS

Pull Buoy—This buoyant piece of equipment is placed between a swimmer's thighs and allows the hips and legs to ride higher in the water without kicking. It is a good tool to use to increase the force work on the upper body (since you are not kicking) or to give your legs a rest. Many triathletes utilize the pull buoy to simulate wetsuit swimming. But, if used too much, this training device can be detrimental. While intermittent use of the pull buoy is a good addition to your swim workout, a steady diet of it can lead to poor form. Too much pull buoy work can reinforce an incorrect body position, one that rides too high and too flat in the water.

Fins—When used periodically while doing drill work, fins are great aids to simulate fast swimming, increase ankle flexibility, and perfect your kick. Using the fins when performing drills allows you to focus on the specifics of the drill at hand, rather than expending energy to maintain a steady kick to keep your body correctly positioned.

Fin Socks—These are neoprene socks worn to prevent blisters when you wear fins.

Fist Gloves—These gloves have no finger slots and are slipped over your hands while they are clenched in a fist. These aids are utilized during the turns, you may choose to add a few quick dolphin kicks for extra propulsion prior to rotating.

Rotation—As you leave the wall, you begin your rotation, keeping your body in-line, rotating over so that you are facing the bottom of the pool. You should be fully rotated onto your stomach as you reach the surface of the pool.

Swim—Once you are on your stomach, begin your kick, initiate your first pull, and you are off!

This may seem like a difficult series of movements, but with some persistence, you will be completing flawless flip turns in no time. First, you should just practice somersaulting in the water, completing steps 1 through 4 in the prescribed sequence. Rather than hitting the wall with your feet, as in step 4, continue your flipping motion, maintaining your streamline, continuing all the way around, until you are standing upright in the water. Turn around, push off the bottom of

---

Fist Drill to promote the "grabbing" of the water with your forearm as well as high elbow catch.

Tennis Balls—These can be gripped in each hand and create the same effect as the fist gloves.

Wooden Dowel or PVC Pipe—These should be about 6 to 8 inches long and are used in a variation of the Catch-up Drill. With each arm cycle, you grab the dowel or pipe with one hand while releasing it with the other.

Hand Paddles/Web-Fingered Gloves—These are great tools for a force workout, which helps to develop strength. You need to maintain good form with these by concentrating on a slow, high elbow catch and then quicken your stroke through the pull. Remember to use your whole forearm, not just the paddle/glove to "grab" the water on the pull. Too much paddle/glove work can stress the shoulders and lead to injury. So, as with the majority of these swimming aids, use them to supplement your training, but do not overuse.

Kickboard—Kickboards are okay to use for an easy kick that can be sustained while conversing with your lane mate. But, if relied on too much, a kickboard will reinforce an improper body position. Use this tool sparingly and do the majority of your kick sets without a board.

the pool, take a few more strokes, and somersault again. Repeat this drill until you feel comfortable with the flip and then take it into the wall. Remember to tuck quickly, exhale through your nose, roll tightly, land squarely, push off in a streamline, and rotate in-line. Soon you will have mastered the flip turn.

If you live in an area where you do not have access to a swim coach or an organized swim program, you can purchase one of the many swim-stroke videos on the market. Or, see if you can locate a swim clinic that you can attend that will introduce you to proper freestyle stroke technique and to the proper techniques in swimming the other three strokes. Use the off-season to refine your stroke and, by incorporating drills into every workout session, you will be on your way to a more efficient stroke and a more enjoyable swim experience this season.

SWIM TERMS

Building—Gradually increase the pace with each length swum.

Descending—Start off at an easy pace and make each repeat faster than the last, making your last repeat the fastest of the set.

Easy Swim—Low effort, focusing on perfect form.

Fast Swim—As hard an effort as you can make, while maintaining perfect form.

IM—Individual swim medley (butterfly, backstroke, breaststroke, freestyle).

Interval—The period of time that includes the swim effort and the rest interval. For example, 4 × 50s on a 1-minute interval might mean that your 50 swim time is 45 seconds and thus you will have 15 seconds of rest. You will start the next 50 repeat after a total minute elapses (swim plus rest).

Rest Interval—The non-swimming break between repetitions or sets.

Streamline Kick—Extend your arms out above your head with hands overlapped. Your upper arms should cover your ears as you stretch out to be as long as you can. Can be done on your back or stomach.

Swim—Freestyle.

SUGGESTED FREESTYLE SWIM DRILLS

Single-Arm

Keep one arm extended forward, keeping it still and riding high in the water, while you stroke with the other arm. This drill allows you to work on your "pull." Be sure to breathe on your pulling-arm side. Again, imagine you are reaching over a barrel, bending your elbow in the beginning of the pull to initiate a powerful pull. Switch arms after each pool length.

This drill can also be completed with the stationary arm at your side (see Photo 5.4). With one arm at your side, breathe toward that side (the non-pulling side). After swimming a pool length, switch arms. Things to concentrate on in this drill: As your body rotates, your head follows to breathe and then returns to its neutral position.

5.1

5.2

5.3

5.4

Fist

Swim with your fingers closed into a fist. (You can also swim with a tennis ball in each hand.) This drill helps promote elbow-bending in the beginning of the pull and promotes "catching" water through the pull.

5.5

5.6

5.7

Catch-up (also called Touch-and-Go)

This is an alternating single-arm drill. Wait for your hand to meet the other in front before pulling (touch-and go) with the other arm. This drill works on your pull and rotation.

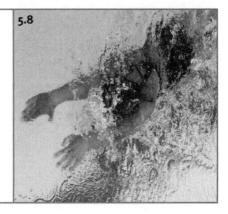

5.8

Catch-up with a Stick

This is similar to regular catch-up, except that you hold a wooden dowel or PVC pipe (4 to 5 inches long) in your hand and, with each arm cycle, grab the dowel with one hand and release with the other. This drill works on centerline entry of your hand, pull, and rotation.

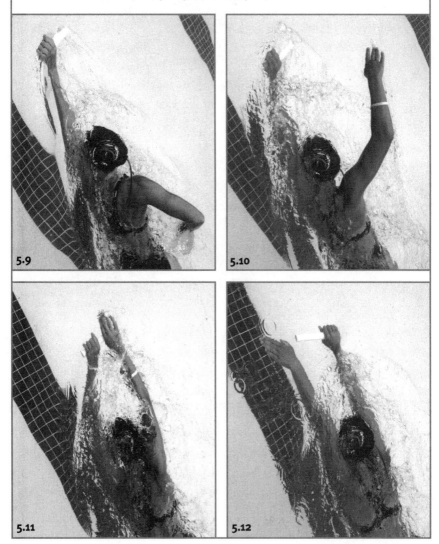

5.9

5.10

5.11

5.12

Fingertip Drag

On your recovery, drag your fingertips lightly across the water before plunging them into the water for the next pull. This drill will work on keeping your elbows high on the recovery.

5.13

5.14

Zipper

During the recovery portion of your stroke, run your thumb along your body from your thigh to your armpit on each stroke. This drill will help you to keep your elbows high during the recovery and it also should help with body rotation.

5.15

5.16

5.17

Skull

Face down, arms stretched out, palms together, and thumbs up. Rotate hands so that thumbs are down and "push" water out just past shoulder width. Rotate hands to thumbs-up position and "push" water back in (similar to a figure eight). "Feel" the water on the entire length of your arms from the tips of your fingers to your armpits, and this skulling movement should move you forward in the pool. Keep your face in the water and raise your head just a bit to breathe while kicking. This drill promotes getting a "feel" for the water.

5.18

5.19

5.20

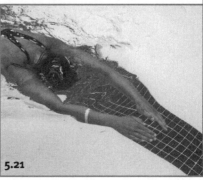

5.21

Tarzan (also called the Lifeguard Swim)

Swim with your head out of the water, keeping it still and looking forward. This drill will help you keep your elbows high during the recovery phase, will help you focus on center-line entry (you can easily see if your stroke is crossing over), and will strengthen the muscles in your neck that you will use while sighting in an open-water swim.

Kick on Side

Kick on your side with both arms at your side. Play with head position and see how that affects how your hips ride in the water. (Think down-hill—head pushing down and out and your hips will ride high.) Be sure to kick from the hip, keeping your toes pointed. This drill works on help-ing you achieve proper body position and a strong, fluid kick.

Kick on Side with Rotation

Same as previous, except after a six-beat kick, roll to your other side. You will initiate the rotation with your hips and core (the shoulders and upper body will follow). This drill focuses on achieving proper body position, balance, and rotation.

5.25

5.26

5.27

5.28

Kick on Side, Arm Out

Lie on your side and kick with your bottom arm extended, riding high in the water with your top arm at your side. Play with your head position, as with the "kick on side" drill, and focus on getting your hips to ride high in the water. Concentrate on feeling long and kick from the hip, keeping your toes pointed. This drill focuses on achieving proper body position and a strong, fluid kick.

Kick on Side, Arm Out with Rotation

Same as previous, except after a six-beat kick, take a pull and recover (one stroke cycle) and roll over to your other side. Lead the rotation with your hips, not your shoulders. This drill focuses on balancing your body position properly, achieving a strong pull, and rotating correctly.

5.29

5.30

5.31

SUGGESTED BUTTERFLY, BACKSTROKE, AND BREASTSTROKE DRILLS

As with freestyle, there are many drills that will help you develop a technically sound stroke in these other stroke areas. Different drills will focus on different aspects of each stroke, and the ones noted in this chapter are good choices to include while first learning the new strokes. So, spice up your swim workouts during the off-season, challenge yourself, and learn one or all of the "other" strokes—your freestyle muscles will be glad that you did.

Butterfly—One-Arm, Two-Arm Combination

Start by taking three one-arm strokes (non-active arm is stationary and extended in front) from a push-off, then switch arms, take three butterfly strokes, and repeat the sequence. Get into a good rhythm while focusing on maintaining a straight line—head-to-shoulders-to-hips body alignment.

Backstroke—One-Arm, Two-Arm Combination

Start by taking three backstrokes (left-right-left) from the push-off, then three right-arm strokes (non-active arm is by your side), then three backstrokes (right-left-right), then three left-arm strokes, and repeat the sequence. Focus on hip and shoulder rotation.

Breaststroke—One-Pull, Two-Kick Combination

Start by taking a full pull from the push-off, then take two kicks, followed by one pull, repeating the sequence. Focus on maintaining body alignment (as noted in the butterfly drill) and a strong pull.

SUGGESTED SWIM SETS

The workouts that follow use abbreviated forms to indicate distance and repetitions. For example "10 × 100 by 25s" translates into 10 repetitions of 100 meters/yards, divided into 25-meter/yard segments of various strokes/exercises. Or "200 swim/200 kick/200 pull" means 200 meters/yards of each form indicated. The sidebar on page 58 offers basic swimming definitions.

WORKOUT 1: **Base Basics**

This workout builds a solid aerobic base for the athlete, while focusing on body rotation (catch-up and left-side/right-side kick), high elbow recovery (fingertip drag), hand entry (catch-up), and a solid pull (fist).

Warm-up
200 swim/200 kick streamline/200 pull

Drill Set
10 × 100 by 25s done as:

25 catch-up/25 fingertip drag/25 fist/25 swim

15-second rest interval between the 100s

Kick Set
9 × 75 done as:

#1–3   25 left-side kick/25 right-side kick/25 swim

#4–6   50 left-side–right-side six-beat kick/25 swim

#7–9   50 left-side–right-side three-beat kick/25 swim

15-second rest interval between the 75s

Swim Set
3 × 200 pull descending

200s on 10-second rest interval

Cool-down
200 easy swim, mixing up strokes

Workout Total: 3,075 yards/meters

WORKOUT 2: **Pace Change and Form**

This workout focuses on good body position, a smooth, balanced kick (streamline kicking without a board), and change of pace.

Warm-up

8 × 75 done as:

50 swim/25 kick with board, straight through, building pace with each 75

Drill Set

10 × 100 by 50s done as:

50 catch-up with stick/50 swim

15-second rest interval between the 100s

Kick Set

8 × 50 done as:

25 streamline kick on your front/

25 streamline kick on your back (no board)

20-second rest interval between 50s

Swim Set

12 × 75 done as:

#1–4   50 easy/25 fast

#5–9   25 easy/25 fast/25 easy

#10–12 50 fast/35 easy

10-second rest between each 75

Cool-down

100 swim/100 pull/100 swim

Workout Total: 3,200 yards/meters

WORKOUT 3: **Short and Fast Form**

This workout focuses on balancing out your stroke (single-arm swims), good body position, a smooth, balanced kick (left-side/right-side kick), and swimming fast while maintaining good form.

Warm-up

5 × 100, building each 100

15-second rest interval

Drill Set

10 × 100 by 25s done as:

25 right-arm

25 left-arm

25 catch-up

25 smooth swim

Kick Set

3 × 100s done as:

25 right-side kick (bottom arm extended out)

25 left-side kick (bottom arm extended out)

50 left-side/right-side six-beat kick

20-second rest interval

Swim Set

10 × 50

Select an interval that you can hold for each 50—1 minute to 1 minute, 20 seconds

10 × 25

Select an interval that you can hold for each 25—45 to 55 seconds

Cool-down

500 easy pull

Workout Total: 3,050 yards/meters

WORKOUT 4: **Short and Fast Form**

This workout focuses on breaking down the other strokes—fly, back-stroke, breaststroke, freestyle—using the drills and then pulling them together for a solid aerobic workout.

Warm-up
4 × 125 descending

15-second rest interval

Drill Set
12 × 50 done as:

#1–3   25 drill/25 swim (fly)

#4–6   25 drill/25 swim (back)

#7–9   25 drill/25 swim (breast)

#10–12 25 drill/25 swim (free)

Kick Set
9 × 75 done as:

25 fly/25 back/25 breast (with board)

20-second rest interval between 75s

Swim Set
8 × 100 IM

20-second rest interval between 100s

Cool-down
500 easy swim

Workout Total: 3,075 yards/meters

S W I M   R E S O U R C E S

www.sportnationvideo.com—This is a great site for swim videos and books for coaches, athletes, and swimmers of all levels.

www.kastawayswimwear.com—This site offers a full array of swim gear, from swimsuits and training equipment to pool products and educational books and videos.

www.usms.org—The United States Masters Swimming site includes information about masters swim clubs, places to swim, discussion forums, articles, workouts, and more.

R E F E R E N C E S

Katz, Jane. *Swimming for Total Fitness: A Progressive Aerobic Program.* With Nancy P. Bruning. New York: Doubleday, Main Street Books, 1993.

Kostich, Alex. "Top 10 Elements of a Perfect Freestyle Stroke, Parts 1 and 2." www.active.com/story.cfm?story_id=8559&sidebar=14&category =swimming

Kostich, Alex. "Learn to master the flip turn to get the most out of your swim workouts." www.active.com/story.cfm?story_id=8152&sidebar =14&category=swimming

Laughlin, Terry. "Off-Season Swim Efficiency." *Triathlete,* December 2003, 42–46.

Luebbers, Mat. "The Freestyle Flip Turn: The Steps to a Freestyle Flip Turn." www.swimming.about.com/cs/techniquetips/a/flipturn_2.htm/

Cycling:
SPIN TO WIN

Just as you focus on perfect technique in the pool and work on drills to improve efficiency on the run, you should also hone your pedaling technique in the off-season. This chapter will examine your various off-season cycling options and discuss how you can use them to improve your performance on the bike.

If you live in a part of the country where the weather prohibits productive outdoor riding in your off-season, indoor training is a foregone conclusion. But even when you have a choice, there are a number of sound reasons to train inside.

THE BENEFITS OF INDOOR CYCLING

- It provides a break from the endless hours spent training on the road.
- It provides you with another cycling option when the weather is too nasty.
- It offers a controlled environment for fitness testing, altering your position, or trying new equipment.
- It provides a controlled setting to work on specific skills.
- It provides a controlled setting to measure performance gains or losses.
- It is a great option when you are short on time or daylight hours.

- It provides a safe, controlled, uninterrupted setting (no stoplights, cars, dogs) for specific intense workouts.
- It provides a social training environment.
- It provides extra motivation via music, training videos, race videos, training partners, or an instructor.

INDOOR TRAINING TOOLS

Once you decide to train indoors, you have many options, varying in price and ranging from simple to high-tech, including trainers, rollers, CompuTrainer, Velotron, and spinning bikes.

Trainers

Trainers (see Photo 6.1) are a convenient, low-cost option for indoor bike training. (Depending upon the shape of your current rear skewer, you may need to purchase a new one that fits correctly into the trainer.) All you need to do is attach your current bike to the trainer by the rear axle, and you are set to ride. There are many makes and models of trainers on the market, and they all create resistance on your rear wheel in one of three ways: magnetic, fluid, and air. Magnetic and fluid models provide a quieter ride than the air models, which are generally less expensive. Some models have the ability to control the resistance on the rear wheel via a cable that is hooked up to a handlebar-control unit. Others have a remote tension adjustment (located on the drive roller), and the simplest have one resistance setting, allowing you to use your gears to simulate terrain changes.

6.1

Trainers are simple to use, fold up for easy storage, are relatively inexpensive, and do not take up a lot of space. They are a wonderful option to use for testing, performing specific workouts, recovery rides, and working on pedaling efficiency.

Rollers

Rollers (see Photo 6.2) consist of three revolving drums on which you ride your bike. They offer a challenging option for indoor training because

unlike trainers, your bike is not locked in. You must focus on smooth pedaling, while balancing the bike as if on the road. Rollers provide instant feedback, for if your stroke gets choppy or you do not maintain your balance, you may find yourself sprawled on the floor. Rollers are great for maintaining an "on-the-road" feel during the off-season and creating a smooth pedal stroke. However, there is a bit of a learning curve, so proceed carefully.

CompuTrainer

The CompuTrainer (see Photo 6.3) is a trainer/ergometer that works with Windows PC software, providing the user with programmed courses, the ability to create and download courses, *SpinScan* (electronic pedal stroke analysis software), performance-data display (instant/average/peak for watts, cadence, heart rate and speed plus distance, lead, lap-time, finish-time, and calories), and modem-racing software.

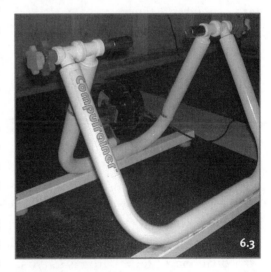

A terrific way to smooth out your pedal stroke is to utilize the *SpinScan* option of the CompuTrainer. The *SpinScan* is a graphic display of your pedaling stroke. Your left and right legs are isolated, and the scan breaks the stroke into segments, displaying all of this on your computer monitor. By pedaling in the *SpinScan* mode, you can vary left–right leg output and force application to the pedal and see immediately what the result is.

The CompuTrainer, although more costly than a basic trainer, is a great tool to use for measuring performance improvement, perfecting pedal stroke, simulating riding on real race courses, and completing specific workouts (hill climbing, intervals, time trials, recovery rides). And with its interactive capabilities, it is an enjoyable option for indoor training.

Velotron

The Velotron (see Photo 6.4), manufactured by the same company as the CompuTrainer (RacerMate, Inc.), is a computer-controlled, electronic bicycle ergometer that works with Windows PC software. Its high-tech design provides laboratory-grade accuracy, 24 gear ratios, high durability with low maintenance, and a road-like ride. As with the CompuTrainer, it offers simulated courses, performance-data display (average and peak values for watts, cadence, heart rate, speed, distance, calories, and time), data recording and graphing, biomechanical feedback, and computer-controlled

6.4

watts/time exercise sessions. It has a broader load-range than the CompuTrainer (5 to 2000 watts) and tops out as the most expensive option for indoor training.

The Velotron comes in several different models: the Pro, which comes with a fully adjustable frame; the Elite, which comes with a standard bike frame; and the Basic, for which you supply your own bike frame. If you are looking for a high-tech training toy with all the bells and whistles and that provides a road-like feel in the comfort of your own home, the Velotron is for you.

Spinning Bikes

What is the difference between "Spinning" and "indoor cycling"? Spinning is a brand name for the indoor cycling program developed by Johnny G., the pioneer of Spinning. An indoor cycling class that is offered as a "Spinning" class must utilize the official Spinner bike and the instructor has to be Johnny G.-certified. Different fitness centers and clubs may also have their own specific indoor cycling programs using bikes similar to the Spinner bike and instructors certified by other programs.

What all of the different indoor cycling programs have in common is that they use similar bikes, which have a fixed gear, and a heavy flywheel with adjustable resistance (see Photo 6.5). There are lots of different makes and models (they are also available for home use and vary in price), and the bikes can be adjusted for a comfortable fit, as opposed to the usual stationary bikes found in fitness centers and gyms. The saddle is adjustable both up-and-down and fore-and-aft. The handlebars can be raised and lowered, and most come equipped with aerobars. The pedals generally accommodate road or mountain bike shoes or have pedals with straps for use with training shoes.

The benefits an athlete derives from spinning are several. The continuous motion of the flywheel, and thus the pedals, helps keep your pedaling stroke smooth—no coasting. Spinning classes can also give you the needed motivation and support of others to complete your winter workout. However, you need to be aware of the type of class that is being offered. Often the classes become "hammer-fests," and a steady diet of these high-intensity workouts during the off-season can lead to early season burnout. Do not be tempted to go with the flow when the workout does not match your training schedule. If the workout becomes too intense, back off of the flywheel tension, focus on pedaling economy, and enjoy the company of the other riders.

For the self-disciplined who can afford it, having a spin-bike at home makes it easy for you to jump on it for a workout. There is no set-up time, as there is when hooking up your bike to a trainer or computer monitor. It is always there, waiting, so there can be no excuses for not completing your scheduled ride.

Tips for Setting Up Your Indoor Training Area

Boredom is often what athletes who must train indoors complain about most. As with all of your workouts, you should have a plan for each of your indoor sessions. Have your training area set up and ready to go so that you do not cut into your training time trying to pull every-thing together. Be creative, have fun, and find ways to make these workouts something you look forward to rather than dread.

- Purchase a protective fitness mat to place under your bicycle to prevent sweat from pooling on your floor or carpet. An old rug or towel will work and afterward all you have to do is to throw it in the wash for an easy cleanup.
- If using a trainer, place a wooden block or telephone book under the front wheel to level the bike. You can also buy specific risers that will do the same. To simulate hill climbing, increase the thickness of the block.
- Make sure to have at least one fan on to keep you cool. You can use an oscillating floor or wall-mounted fan or a box fan tilted upward.
- When on your training/racing bike, be sure to cover your headset and top tube with a towel and have another on hand with which to wipe yourself off.
- Make sure that you have plenty of fluid on hand to drink so that you stay properly hydrated.
- Have a good music system at hand and use a CD player with a "repeat" function to keep your session uninterrupted.
- Use your TV/VCR/DVD system to watch TV and play movies, triathlon races, cycling races, and training videos.
- Use a large whiteboard to write your workouts on so that you can easily follow the plan for the day.

OUTDOOR TRAINING TOOLS

Fixed-Gear Bikes

Fixed-gear bikes are the road equivalent to spinning bikes. They are single-speed bikes without a freewheel; and whenever the bike is moving, the pedals will continue to go around—there is no coasting on a fixed-gear bike. If interested in fixed-gear riding, you will need to convert an old road bike. Converting it is not that difficult or costly. Your best bet is to take it to your local bike shop and have them remove the derailleurs and shifters and put on an appropriate hub. You should choose a gear (generally a range of 39–42 × 15–19) that puts you at about 90 rpm on the flats when riding easily.

The benefits of riding a fixed-gear bike are many. Riding one can improve your pedaling efficiency by forcing you to keep pedaling when you might otherwise coast—you will get a high-quality work-out in less time. On the flats, you can practice smooth, consistent pedal strokes with no chance to coast—your legs will always be in motion. Downhill riding will cause you to automatically speed up your cadence, and you must focus on a smooth stroke or you will find yourself bouncing on the saddle. Riding a fixed-gear bike will also make you a stronger rider, for when you hit an uphill, you will have no choice but to work harder (no gear changes) to get up and over. Fixed-gear bikes require some additional caution, especially while turning, as you will need to take the safest angle so a pedal does not hit the pavement.

Remember that it will take a bit of practice to become comfortable on a fixed-gear bike, and it is advisable to stick to fairly straight and flat or gently rolling terrain. So, if you have an old clunker collecting dust, break it out and convert it to a fixed-gear bike. Come race season, you will notice the difference.

PowerCranks

PowerCranks are patented bicycle cranks that turn independently from each other (see Photo 6.6). These innovative training tools provide instant feedback, for if you do not maintain constant pressure on the cranks (not "pedaling in circles"), you will find both pedals at the bottom of the pedaling stroke. They focus on the major hip flexor and hamstring muscles, while also improving your pedal stroke. PowerCranks can help to balance out your pedal stroke, preventing a strong leg from compensating for a weak leg—the weak leg will have to work to keep up with the stronger. They also provide a great aerobic workout, while continually focusing on an efficient and economical pedal stroke. And, as an added bonus, users claim that PowerCranks have a positive effect on their running due to the increased strength in their hip flexors and a faster turnover.

These cost between $690 and $825 new (used ones are available) and need to be installed on your bike. They take a bit of practice to get used to and can be ridden on the road or on a trainer. PowerCranks can be a great supplement to your training, especially in the off-season, and can help you achieve a more economical pedaling stroke and build up your aerobic engine.

DEVELOPING A BETTER PEDAL STROKE

What constitutes an economical pedal stroke? Being able to apply force to the pedals for 360 degrees! Studies from the United States Olympic Training Center have found that most of a cyclist's power is produced during the downstroke, from about three o'clock to five o'clock. This leaves a huge area for improvement for increased efficiency at the top and bottom of the stroke. You must train your nervous system and muscles to apply force all the way around the pedal stroke. By practicing pedaling skills, you will improve the communication between your nervous system and your muscles. Continued focused attention on improving your stroke should yield a more economical stroke. By improving your pedaling stroke, you will also improve your endurance (increased efficiency of the stroke conserves energy) and you will improve your speed (there will be increased power on each revolution).

Becoming an economical pedaler will not happen overnight. You must devote a significant amount of time to improve your pedal stroke so that it becomes an unconscious, natural movement. One of the most effective and efficient ways to do this is to incorporate pedaling-specific drills into your workout sessions, and the best time to start is during the off-season. These can be stand-alone workouts, or you can build them into your warm-up leading into other sessions. These drill workouts (one-legged drills, one-leg focus, spin-ups, and high cadence) are best performed on a trainer, but they can also be completed on the road, once you have perfected the skill.

Cycling Drills

Isolating Each Leg—To begin, place a chair or stool on each side of your bicycle, on which you will rest your non-active leg. Warm up, spinning, for 10 to 15 minutes, and then place one foot on the chair/stool. Be sure that you remain squarely seated on the saddle and do not allow your hips to drop. Start your form sessions with a short interval (20 to 30 seconds), pedaling smoothly with one leg and then switching to the other leg. Focus on applying force on the top and bottom portions of your pedal stroke. (These should be the areas where you experience the greatest difficulty.) After a few repetitions, you should begin to feel fatigue in your hip flexors and along the front of your shin. Once you become too fatigued to perform the drill with perfect form, it is time to stop.

The motion of the stroke should feel as if you are sliding your foot forward inside your shoe as you clear the top of the stroke and begin pushing down, and then sliding your foot back inside your shoe across the bottom of the stroke (similar to scraping mud off your shoe). As you are pedaling, think "up and back and forward and down." If you hear a clunking sound as you are pedaling, you know that you are not applying force evenly through the entire 360 degrees. This unsettling noise occurs when a somewhat slack chain (loss of force causes the slackening) is suddenly tightened to create increased tension in the chain (appropriate use of force). Look down at your chain while pedaling. If you notice some slack in the chain during your pedal stroke, that is a sign that you are not applying tension on the chain and thus not applying force throughout the entire stroke. Correct force on the entire pedal stoke will result in consistent chain tension and a smooth, quiet stroke.

Make sure that during your one-legged sessions you begin pedaling at a cadence that will allow you to concentrate fully on correct form. Gradually increase your cadence as your form improves and hold your interval for as long as you can keep good form (quiet, smooth strokes). You can start with 20- to 30-second intervals per leg and work up to 1-minute intervals.

One-Leg Focus—You can also perform one-legged drills with both feet still clipped into the pedals. To complete this drill, concentrate on working just one leg, while relaxing and unweighting the other. Pedal for a specific time interval and then switch to the other leg. As with any one-legged drills, focus on applying force evenly around the entire pedal stroke.

Spin-Ups—After a warm-up, complete repeats of 15 to 20 seconds, steadily building to a maximal cadence—you should just start to bounce on the saddle. Spin easy for recovery and then repeat the spin-up. Make note of your high cadence and aim to better this during each session.

High Cadence—As with the spin-ups, build your cadence to a maximal level. Once you hit the bounce stage, back down a bit and hold this high, good-form cadence for a certain time interval. You can start with repeats of 30 seconds of high cadence, followed by 30 seconds of your normal cadence for recovery, building to 1-minute high cadence with 1-minute normal cadence for recovery.

Specific Drill Workouts

Here are some proven pedaling drills that should find their way into your off-season training routines. These can be stand-alone form sessions or can be used as part of your warm-up, leading into a more intense session. You may have to alter the work and rest intervals to suit your particular fitness and strength levels. Also, when first attempting these drill sessions, your gear selection should be fairly easy. As your technique and strength improve, adjust your gears accordingly.

WORKOUT 1: **One-Legged Drill Session**

Warm-up

10–15 minutes of easy spinning

Drill Set

- 30 seconds right leg, 30 seconds left leg.
- 30 seconds both legs, focusing on proper form at a comfortable cadence. (Aim to build the interval to 1 minute as your form and fitness improve.)
- Repeat three times through.
- 5 minutes of easy spinning and repeat the sequence.

Cool-down

10–15 minutes of easy spinning.

Workout Total: Approximately 44 minutes

WORKOUT 2: **One-Leg Focus Pyramid Session**

Warm-up

10–15 minutes of easy spinning

Drill Set

- 30 seconds right leg/15 seconds both legs.
- 30 seconds left leg/15 seconds both legs.
- 45 seconds right leg/15 seconds both legs.
- 45 seconds left leg/15 seconds both legs.
- 60 seconds right leg/15 seconds both legs.
- 60 seconds left leg/15 seconds both legs.

Repeat pyramid three times through.

Cool-down

10 – 15 minutes of easy spinning

Workout Total: Approximately 48 minutes

WORKOUT 3: **Spin-up Drill Session**

Warm-up

10–15 minutes of easy spinning

Drill Set

- Spin at your normal cadence for 45 seconds and then spin-up as high as you can for 15 seconds. Make note of your highest cadence and try to better it with each repetition and with each workout.
- Repeat this sequence four times.
- 5 minutes easy spinning and repeat spin-ups.

Cool-down

10–15 minutes of easy spinning

Workout Total: Approximately 44 minutes

WORKOUT 4: **High Cadence Drill Session**

Warm-up

10–15 minutes of easy spinning

Drill Set

- Spin at your normal cadence for 1 minute and then 1 minute at your max cadence (good form, no bouncing).
- Repeat this sequence three times.
- 5 minutes easy spinning and repeat high cadence repeats.

Cool-down

10–15 minutes of easy spinning

Workout Total: Approximately 47 minutes

CYCLING RESOURCES

www.powercranks.com — This is the home Web site for everything that you want to know about PowerCranks.

www.spinning.com — This is the official site for Johnny G. Spinning.

www.computrainer.com — This is the official site for CompuTrainer and Velotron.

www.fixedgeargallery.com — This is a great link with photos of fixed-gear bikes and links to fixed-gear resources.

http://bikefarmer.com — This is an online portal where you can find rollers, trainers, and other bike equipment.

www.indoor-group-cycling.com — This is a site containing a complete line of indoor spinning bikes for home use.

REFERENCES

Brown, Sheldon. "Fixed Gear for the Road."
www.sheldonbrown.com/fixed.html

Carmichael, Chris. "Pedaling Technique and Efficiency."
www.roadcycling.com/training/pedalingtechnique.shtml

Friel, Joe. "Training Tips: Two Wheeled Elegance."
www.pikespeakvelo.com/coaching/2wheelelegance.shtml

Gootman, Jason, and Will Kirousis. "Making the Most of Winter."
www.trikats.com

———. "Pedaling Optimization." www.trikats.com

McCormack, Michael. "The Zen of Pedaling."
www.triathloncoach.com/articles/pedal.html

CHAPTER

Running:
EFFICIENCY IS THE KEY

Have you ever had your run form videotaped and/or critiqued? If not, you should, because "cleaning up" your form is one way to gain "free" speed. Unnecessary or inefficient movements during running waste energy. The best way to improve your form and efficiency is by incorporating drill work into your running routine. By breaking down your running motion into distinct movements and performing drills to improve each of these movements, you can greatly increase your efficiency and form, which will in turn improve your speed. Drill work can also help you to develop run-specific strength, agility, coordination, and flexibility. Specific run drills and exercises can easily be incorporated into your run warm-up or they can be completed as a stand-alone form session.

Drill work can be performed anywhere, so be disciplined this off-season and add drill work to your running routine and watch the seconds disappear from your mile split!

SUGGESTED RUN FORM EXERCISES

All of the following exercises can be performed on a track, road, field, or indoor surface. Once you have become proficient, try them on a soft, grassy surface without shoes. This will add a new dimension to your running, increasing flexibility and building strength in muscles not often used due to the supportive nature of running shoes.

Walking Lunge

Assume a lunge position, keeping the forward thigh parallel to the ground. Make sure that your forward knee does not move past your toe, as this will stress the knee. Your back leg is extended behind. Step forward into another lunge, looking straight ahead, chest up, and move your arms in conjunction with your legs. (As your one leg steps forward, the arm on the opposite side of your body is also driven forward.)

Benefit: This exercise stretches the hip flexors, while improving leg drive, and strengthens the glutes and hamstrings.

High Knee Lift

Rise up onto your toes and, as you step forward, lift one thigh so that it is parallel to the ground and then repeat with the other leg. Look forward, keep your back straight and upper body relaxed, and coordinate your arm movement with your leg movement, as in the lunge drill.

Benefit: This exercise will help strengthen your calves, hip flexors, and ankles and will also improve your posture.

Twisting Lunge

This movement is similar to the walking lunge, but as you step, extend your upper body over your front left leg, while taking your left elbow down toward the inside left ankle. Step and repeat the same movement with the right leg and arm.

Benefit: This exercise helps to develop hamstring strength, while also stretching your hip flexors and lower back.

Toe Walk

With each step, rise up onto the toes of your forward foot—step, rise, and repeat.

Benefit: This exercise develops lower leg strength, while also stretching the Achilles tendon.

Grapevine

Begin by moving your right leg across your body in front of your left foot. Step laterally with your left leg and then move your right leg across, behind your left leg, and repeat the sequence. After one repetition in this direction, change so that your left leg is the lead leg—i.e., move your left leg across in front of your right leg, step laterally with your right leg, and then bring your left leg across behind your right leg and repeat.

Benefit: This exercise helps to develop your lower limb strength, agility, and flexibility.

High Skips

Just like when you were a kid, swing your arms forward forcefully and skip as high as you can, driving up off of the foot touching the ground.

Benefit: This exercise helps build explosive power in your running stride.

Striders

Striders are "slow-motion" sprints where you focus on your leg turnover (cadence), working to achieve a quiet, relaxed upper body and quick, light steps. This motion is not all-out, but rather a controlled fast movement where your forefoot strikes the ground first (see Photo 7.13), and not heel first (see Photo 7.14). You should aim for at least 90 foot strikes per minute.

Benefit: This exercise helps develop a quicker cadence and also helps develop good posture while running.

Downhill Running

Perform these runs on a slight incline on a soft surface (grass or dirt). Utilize gravity to "pull" you down the hill. Drop your center of gravity a bit by lowering your arms and take short, quick steps, minimizing contact with the ground. Overstriding will cause you to strike with your heel, creating a braking action with each step.

Benefit: This motion will help you work on a faster leg turnover and a proper foot strike.

SUGGESTED STAND-ALONE FORM WORKOUT

WORKOUT 1: **Stand-Alone Form Workout**

On the Track
10-minute easy run

On the Straightaways
- Perform the drills in the order listed below and walk back to the start for your recovery before starting the next drill.
- Grapevine—switch lead leg every tenth crossover
- High skips
- Walking lunges
- Jogging backward
- Toe walk
- Striders—four to six repeats
- 5- to 10-minute easy run, cool-down, and light stretch

Workout Total: Approximately 30 minutes

Note: You can incorporate any of the drills listed in this chapter into a form workout or as a lead-in to any of your run sessions.

RUNNING BAREFOOT

When incorporating barefoot running into your routine, it is important that you increase your running time gradually so that you don't overstress the ligaments and tendons of the foot and lower leg. To prepare yourself for barefoot running, shed your shoes and walk barefoot as often as possible. This will accustom your feet to their new and unsupported environment. After a few walking sessions, start with an easy jog and slowly move into your full running stride. Barefoot running will help strengthen your stabilizing muscles and will allow you to attain greater flexibility with the calf and Achilles tendon. As your foot and lower leg muscles and tendons get stronger, you will become a more efficient runner, incur fewer injuries, and thus enhance your running performance.

The first thing that you should notice when running barefoot is what part of your foot strikes the ground first—the fore- to mid-foot. Barefoot running can help transform heel strikers to mid-foot strikers. With their extensive cushioning, running shoes often give runners a false sense of security. When you run barefoot, your natural strike is the fore- to mid-foot. Landing on your heel while running barefoot is painful and a reminder that we were built to run with a more forward foot strike.

Take the time this off-season to work on your run technique by incorporating drills into your warm-up and by completing one stand-alone drill session each week. Mix and match the drills prior to each run session and focus on one aspect of your running form while completing your drill work—quick leg turnover, quiet upper body, forefoot strike, relaxed upper body, linear arm motion. The drills are simple to perform, will increase your flexibility, help strengthen run-specific muscles, and will make you a more economical runner—which will translate into faster run splits come race season.

RUN   RESOURCES

www.posetech.com—Pose Method of Running (DVD or VHS), Dr. Nicolas Romanov. This video demonstrates the Pose Method and will show you how to run efficiently and save energy, how to run faster following natural biomechanic patterns of movement, and how to run injury free with this new, simple technique.

REFERENCES

Horowitz, Jeff. "Simple Drills Can Clean Up Your Running Form, Efficiency." http://www.active.com/print.cfm?category= running& story_id=9267

Shepherd, John. "Ring in the Old, Ring in the New," *Peak Performance,* August 2003, 6–8.

Yessis, Michael. *Explosive Running: Using the Science of Kinesiology to Improve Your Performance.* Chicago, IL: Contemporary Books, 2000.

C H A P T E R

Cardiovascular Conditioning:

INDOOR TRAINING ALTERNATIVES TO SWIM/BIKE/RUN

If you do not have the luxury of living in an area where year-round outdoor training is an option, or you just hate training in the cold or snow, look beyond the normal treadmill and trainer routines to help you maintain your fitness. An important aspect of your off-season training is variety, and by including alternatives to your winter training, you can avoid the boredom often associated with training indoors. Some indoor options are: deep-water running (also known as aqua-jogging), elliptical trainers, stair-climbers, and rowing ergometers. For those athletes who are fortunate enough to have warm-weather options during the off-season, these indoor alternatives also can and should be incorporated into your winter training plan, as well as throughout your entire season.

DEEP-WATER RUNNING

Deep-water running (DWR) mimics land running with one exception: you're floating. Comparative analyses of deep-water and land-based running have concluded that water running is a satisfactory substitute for regular land-based running to maintain aerobic fitness. One study has shown that competitive runners maintained their VO_2max and 5K times after 4 weeks of deep-water running. Another demonstrated that VO_2max and ventilatory threshold were unchanged after 6 weeks of DWR.

To perform deep-water running properly, you should purchase a vest or belt to ensure that you can keep your head above water. The belt is the preferred choice of flotation, since it tends to fit better than a vest or lifejacket and does not restrict your natural arm movement. You could also utilize a tether cord to keep you in one place, or you can actually "run" laps back and forth across the deep end of the pool.

Often, athletes new to deep-water running feel that the flotation device restricts their breathing and that the pressure from the surrounding water further contributes to this feeling of constriction. This tightness may cause you to breathe more shallowly than usual and thus cause you to be short of breath. Be patient, as it may take a bit of time for you to adapt your new running environment, and you will need to pay close attention to your breathing to make sure that it's deep enough.

You can also complete your deep-water running workouts without a flotation device. This method requires much more strength to keep your body stable and upright. Also, your running form may be compromised, since staying afloat often becomes your primary concern. Although the absence of a constricting belt or vest may alleviate some of the tightness around the chest, it's best to start your water running exercises with a flotation device.

FORM TIPS FOR DEEP-WATER RUNNING

- The water level should hit shoulder height.
- The head should be in a neutral position, mouth out of the water, eyes looking ahead.
- The body should lean slightly forward.
- The arm motion is the same as on land, and hands should be loosely closed, slicing through the water.
- The leg motion should mimic the motion on land. A lower stride cadence may result due to the resistance from the water.

Studies have shown that responses during deep-water running are, on average, 10 to 12 beats lower than those achieved during traditional running at matched submaximal intensities; therefore, use a self-determined rating of perceived exertion (RPE) during workouts (see sidebar in Chapter 3). Otherwise, duplicate in the water those running sessions scheduled on land. If your training plan calls for a 1-hour recovery run on land, do a 1-hour recovery run in the water. To duplicate track intervals on the schedule, do them in the pool at a high intensity with a high turnover rate and rest intervals of easy water jogging in between. (The rest intervals should be shorter since recovery in the water will be much faster than on land.)

Many athletes find deep-water running boring. The key to breaking up the monotony is to vary the workouts. Due to the lack of impact and reduced stress to the body, day-to-day recovery from deep-water running is faster than for traditional running. This means that athletes can deal with more frequent intensity and greater duration in the water than on the track or road.

WORKOUTS FOR DEEP-WATER RUNNING

WORKOUT 1: Base Building Session

Warm-up

10-minute easy jog

Main Set

- 2 minutes straight leg kick; driving from the hip with toes pointed down
- 10-minute steady-state run
- 2 minutes straight leg kick; driving from the hip with toes pointed down
- 10-minute steady-state run
- 2 minutes straight leg kick, driving from the hip with toes pointed down

Cool-down

10-minute easy jog

Workout Total: 46 minutes

WORKOUT 2: **Interval Session**

Warm-up

10-minute easy jog

Main Set

5 × 20 seconds hard, 40 seconds easy

4 to 6 × 90 seconds hard, 3-minute easy rest interval

Cool-down

10-minute easy jog

Workout Total: 43–52 minutes

WORKOUT 3: **Pyramid Session**

Warm-up

10-minute easy jog

Main Set

- 1 minute hard, 1 minute easy
- 2 minutes hard, 2 minutes easy
- 3 minutes hard, 3 minutes easy
- 4 minutes hard, 4 minutes easy
- 5 minutes hard

Cool-down

10-minute easy jog

Workout Total: 45 minutes

(For a longer workout, go back down the pyramid: 5, 4, 3, 2, 1, and cool-down.)

WORKOUT 4: **Drill Session**

Warm-up

10-minute easy jog

Main Set

- 30 seconds at high turnover, quick, short strides with fast arm movement
- 3 minutes easy
- 30 seconds butt-kicks, quick flexion of knee
- 3 minutes easy
- 30 seconds high knee, driving the lead knee as high as possible with fast arm movement
- 3 minutes easy
- 30 seconds straight-leg kick; driving from the hip with toes pointed down

Cool-down

10-minute easy jog

Workout Total: 31 minutes

(For a longer workout, repeat the set and then cool-down.)

ELLIPTICAL TRAINERS

Elliptical trainers are a great indoor alternative to running outdoors and have the added benefit of putting minimal stress on the joints, while offering a weight-bearing activity. The feet of the user never leave the trainer, thus eliminating the pounding of a normal run. You stand in an upright position gently holding onto the machine's handrails (or "pump pole") and stride in either a forward or backward motion (avoid striding backward if you have knee problems). Studies have shown that as we stride forward, the human foot travels in an elliptical pattern, and the trainer mimics this natural motion. Some elliptical trainers offer dual action (upper and lower body), and these machines not only target the large muscle groups of the lower body but also the chest, back, triceps, and biceps—a great total body workout!

A University of Wisconsin study revealed that elliptical trainers produced load forces similar to those of walking, and, as with deep-water running, athletes can adapt their land-based running routine to a similar workout on the trainer. Elliptical trainers are found in most gyms and can also be purchased for home use.

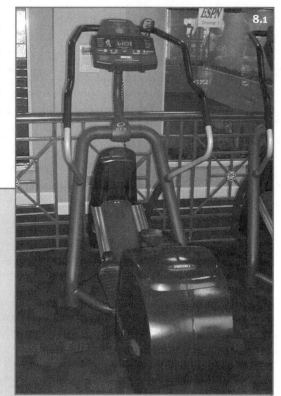

ELLIPTICAL TRAINER TIPS

• Before you start your workout: Read the instructions for the trainer!

• Check out the console and familiarize yourself with the particular features of the trainer.

• Begin slow and become comfortable with the motion of the trainer before you increase your intensity.

• Complete a few manual sessions before you move on to the programmed workouts.

• Have a towel and water bottle handy.

• Grip the handrails lightly.

• Keep good posture.

• Wear appropriate, supportive footwear.

• Include a proper warm-up and cool-down with every session.

SAMPLE WORKOUTS FOR
THE ELLIPTICAL TRAINER

WORKOUT 1: **Base Building Session**

Warm-up
Approximately 10-minutes warm-up, slowly building your effort

Main Set
30–60 minutes of steady aerobic effort on the elliptical trainer

You can mix up forward and backward striding throughout the workout.

Workout Total: 40–70 minutes

WORKOUT 2: **Interval Session**

Warm-up
Approximately 10 minutes, slowly building your effort

Main Set
Complete 3 to 4 × 6-minute repeats, hard effort, with 2-minute recoveries (recoveries can be easy backward striding).

Cool-down
10 minutes of easy striding

Workout Total: 44–50 minutes

WORKOUT 3: Tempo Session

Warm-up
Approximately 10 minutes, slowly building your effort

Main Set
20 minutes steady state, moderate effort

Cool-down
10 minutes, easy striding

Workout Total: 40 minutes

WORKOUT 4: Pyramid Session

Warm-up
Approximately 10 minutes, slowly building your effort

Main Set
- 1 minute hard, 1 minute easy
- 2 minutes hard, 2 minutes easy
- 3 minutes hard, 3 minutes easy
- 2 minutes hard, 2 minutes easy
- 1 minute hard, 1 minute easy

For the "hard" efforts, focus on a quick light stride.

Cool-down
10-minutes of easy striding

Workout Total: 38 minutes

STAIR-CLIMBERS

Stair-climbing is another wonderful indoor aerobic, as well as a lower-body strength training, option to include during your off-season. There are two types of stair-climbing machines: nonmechanized and mechanized. The nonmechanized machines tend to be cheaper, less expensive models that use air pistons to provide resistance. These machines will not allow you to move fast enough to get an adequate aerobic workout and are geared more for low-intensity efforts. The more popular models that are frequently found in gyms and health clubs are the mechanized stair machines. These styles of stair machines include staircase ergometers, independent pedal steppers, and linked pedal steppers. Staircase ergometers (see Photo 8.2), with their escalator-like movement, best mimic true stair-climbing, but offer a higher impact workout than the pedal stepper. On the independent and linked pedal stepper, you stand on two footplates, while gently holding onto handrails. You then alternate pressing one foot

down, while pulling up the other. These two styles of machines are considered nonimpact since the user's feet never leave the footplates. Both the ergometers and steppers have settings for speed, time, distance, and workout intensity.

To get the most out of your stair session, proper form is important. You should stand upright, only holding the handrails lightly for balance. Those who grip the handrails tightly and bend at the waist are

STAIR-CLIMBING TIPS

- Before you start your workout: Read the instructions for the stair-climber!

- Check out the console and familiarize yourself with the particular characteristics of the stepper.

- Know where the shut-off is for the staircase ergometer models.

- Stepping rate: Choose an initial stepping rate that allows you to keep good form.

- Complete a few manual sessions before moving on to the programmed workouts.

- Have a towel and water bottle handy.

- Grip the handrails lightly.

- Keep your posture upright.

- Wear appropriate, supportive footwear.

- Include a proper warm-up and cool-down with every session.

using their arms to support their body rather than using their core muscles to do so. "Cheating" on form prevents users from working their back muscles and also reduces the overall intensity of the workout because the leg muscles are not supporting the full weight of the body.

It is also key that you lift your feet a full "stride" of about 6.5 to 8 inches to fully engage the muscles of the legs, buttocks, and back. Short, choppy steps or tiptoe steps will mainly work the calf muscles and thus will not provide as much benefit as full steps. Improper form—such as bending at the waist, supporting the upper body with shoulders and wrists, short stepping, or tiptoe stepping—not only reduces the benefit of the workout, but can lead to knee, hip, wrist, or lower back discomfort or injury.

SAMPLE WORKOUTS
FOR STAIR-CLIMBING

WORKOUT 1: **Base Building Session**

Warm-up
Approximately 10 minutes, slowly building your effort and step rate

Main Set
30–60 minutes of steady aerobic effort on the climber

Workout Total: 40–70 minutes

WORKOUT 2: **Interval Session**

Warm-up
Approximately 10 minutes, slowly building your effort and step rate

Main Set
Complete 3 to 4 × 6 minutes hard effort, with 2-minute easy step recovery

Cool-down
10 minutes of easy stepping

Workout Total: 44–50 minutes

WORKOUT 3: **Tempo Session**

Warm-up
Approximately 10 minutes, slowly building your effort and step rate

Main Set
20 minutes steady state, moderate effort

Cool-down
10 minutes, easy stepping

Workout Total: 40 minutes

WORKOUT 4: **Pyramid Session**

Warm-up
10 minutes, slowly building your effort and step rate

Main Set
- 1 minute hard, 1 minute easy
- 2 minutes hard, 2 minutes easy
- 3 minutes hard, 3 minutes easy
- 4 minutes hard, 4 minutes easy
- 3 minutes hard, 3 minutes easy
- 2 minutes hard, 2 minutes easy
- 1 minute hard, 1 minute easy

Cool-down
10 minutes of easy stepping

Workout Total: 52 minutes

ROWING ERGOMETERS

Another option for an indoor, low-impact, total-body workout is the rowing ergometer. This indoor workout not only provides a great cardiovascular session but also is a great strength workout. Indoor rowing works the muscles of the legs, back, abdomen, arms, and shoulders and will help to increase the flexibility of the legs, shoulders, and back. Studies show that rowing burns more calories than cycling at the same perceived level of exertion since more muscle groups are involved.

There are several types of rowers on the market and they include those that are powered by piston, air, water, or magnetic resistance. One of the most popular rowing ergometers found in gyms, health clubs, and homes is the Concept2 rowing machine (shown here, Photo 8.3), which utilizes air resistance and provides a quiet, fluid workout.

Five Basic Steps of the Rowing Stroke

The Catch: Your arms should be straight with no bend at the elbows, wrists are flat, your fingers should loosely grip the handle(s), shins are upright, chest is pressed against the thighs, back straight, head is up, and your eyes should be looking ahead.

The Leg Drive: Begin the leg drive by pressing down on your legs while keeping your arms straight and back strong.

The Body Swing: Once the leg drive is finished, gradually bend your arms and swing back with your upper body.

The Finish: The arms have fully taken over from the leg drive and you should pull your elbows back past your body and bring your hands all the way into your lower chest/upper abdomen. Squeezing your shoulder blades together at the finish can help you maintain good form for a long finish.

Recovery: The recovery follows the first four steps in reverse—first straighten your arms, then lean your upper body forward at the hips following your arms; next bend your legs as you slide forward on the seat. These motions should be completed in one fluid movement and at a controlled speed.

ROWING TIPS

- Before you start your workout: Read the instructions!

- Become familiar with the different programs and settings of the model rower that you are using. Some units will have a computerized readout that will tell you your strokes per minute (SPM), time, distance, and calories burned and provide you with pre-built workouts.

- Note your (SPM) of different exertions. About 20–22 SPM is a good starting point.

- Adjust the tension of the flywheel or other mode of resistance before you start.

- Make sure that you work on proper technique to get the most out of your workout and prevent injury.

SAMPLE WORKOUTS
FOR INDOOR ROWING

WORKOUT 1: **Time Trial Session**

Warm-up
Approximately 10 minutes, slowly building your
effort and SPM

Main Set
2,500-meter time trial

Cool-down
10 minutes of easy rowing

WORKOUT 2: **Pyramid Session**

Warm-up
Approximately 10 minutes, slowly building your effort
and strokes per minute (SPM)

Main Set
- 1 minute hard, 1 minute easy
- 2 minutes hard, 1–2 minutes easy
- 3 minutes hard, 2–3 minutes easy
- 6 minutes hard, 3–4 minutes easy
- 2 minutes hard, 2–3 minutes easy
- 1 minute hard

Cool-down
10 minutes of easy rowing

Workout Total: 55–58 minutes

WORKOUT 3: **Speed Work Session**

Warm-up
Approximately 10 minutes, slowly building your effort and SPM

Main Set
- Row 10 strokes as fast and hard as you can every 2 minutes.
- Start with 10 minutes and build to 20 minutes of this pattern.

Cool-down
10 minutes of easy rowing

WORKOUT 4: **Interval Session**

Warm-up
Approximately 10 minutes, slowly building your effort and SPM

Main Set
1,000 meters × 3 at moderate effort

4 minutes easy rowing in between each set

Cool-down
10 minutes of easy rowing

WORKOUT 5: Base Building Session

Warm-up
Approximately 10 minutes, slowly building your effort and SPM

Main Set
3,000 meters at a steady aerobic pace

Repeat one to two times as your endurance increases.

Cool-down
10 minutes of easy rowing

Not only are these indoor training options a good choice during your base periods, they also can be integrated into your yearly training plan. These activities are also great alternatives as recovery workouts throughout the season. You can head to the pool or gym after a hard session on the track or bike for an easy recovery session with one of these low-impact options. For athletes with a high propensity for injury, these low-stress modes of exercise will reduce the chance of incurring the all-too-common overuse injuries. For each of these options, you can mimic your land-based aerobic workout during all phases of your training without the added stress. Remember that with any new workout there may be a period of muscle soreness; therefore, introduce alternative forms of training gradually into your training program.

REFERENCES

Burke, Edmund R. *Off-Season Training for Cyclists.* Boulder, CO: VeloPress, 1997.

Concept 2. "Rowing Technique." www.concept2.com

"Deep-Water Running: When Your Training Should Land You in Deep Water." http://www.pponline.co.uk/encyc/0601.htm

Mercer, John. "Biomechanical Comparison of Deep Water and Treadmill Running." http://www.unlv.edu/faculty/jmercer/dwr/dwr.html

USA Cycling Coaching Staff. *USA Cycling Sport Coach Manual.* Colorado Springs, CO: USA Cycling, Inc., 1999.

CHAPTER

Cardiovascular Conditioning:

OUTDOOR TRAINING ALTERNATIVES TO SWIM/BIKE/RUN

Weather permitting, the following alternatives to the traditional workouts associated with swim/bike/run can also be a great addition to your workout plan. They will add variety to your usual routine, utilize underworked muscles, get you outdoors, and build your aerobic engine.

CROSS-COUNTRY SKIING

For those of you living in snow country, cross-country or Nordic skiing is a great crosstraining activity. Cross-country skiing not only works the large muscle groups of the lower body, but also the muscles of the upper body, arms, and lower back. Besides developing total body strength, it is also a productive way to develop your aerobic engine with minimal impact to your joints.

The sport has evolved over the years from just bushwhacking through the woods on a pair of wooden slats to several different styles of skiing: skate (freestyle), classic (diagonal), and ski touring (backcountry).

Skate skiing involves, as the name implies, a skating motion in which the skier glides on the skis on the snow at an angle, while also using his or her poles to move forward. There are three variations of this technique: V1, V2, and V2, Alternate.

V1: The offset pole and one ski hit the snow at the same time. This technique is generally best for steep climbs.

V2: Skiers push off with a double-pole motion for each sidekick. This is the most efficient motion for flats or gradual uphills.

V2, Alternate: Skiers use one double-pole motion for every other sidekick. This motion is best on easy flats and downhills.

Classic skiing technique (diagonal striding) is used on the groomed tracks of ski centers or while making tracks in the backcountry. The motion mimics walking, where the left arm and right leg come forward at the same time and vice versa.

Cross-Country Skiing Equipment

Skis

You first need to decide which type of cross-country skiing you will be doing. The important factor here is where you will be skiing—the ungroomed trails of the backcountry or the machine-groomed track of your local cross-country ski center. A ski developed for the natural surroundings of the backcountry will not perform well on a machine-groomed track and vice versa. Some skis need to be waxed, while others come with a multigrip pattern for traction.

Boots

Boots should fit snugly, but comfortably. Make sure that you try them on with the socks that you will be using during your outings. As with skis, there are different types of boots for the different styles of skiing.

Bindings

Bindings hold the boot to the ski, and again, just as there are different types of skis, there are different types of bindings that match the style of skiing.

Poles

Pole length is dependent upon the style of skiing. Touring poles are sturdier and shorter (reaching to the armpit) than racing-style poles (shoulder height), and skate poles tend to be the tallest (hitting the chin).

Clothing

As with winter cycling or running, layering is a very important aspect of dressing properly for cross-country skiing. You will heat up fast, so be sure not to overdress. Make sure that you have adequate head covering, good gloves, and avoid cotton clothing.

If you are a first-time Nordic skier, make sure that you go to a shop with a knowledgeable staff that can assist you with the correct selection of equipment. Also, schedule a lesson before you take off on your own. Then head out for a great, low-impact, total-body, aerobic workout.

SNOWSHOEING

Another great on-snow option for crosstraining in the off-season is snowshoeing. Just as there have been huge equipment advances for cross-country skiing, so have there been such improvements for snowshoeing. Snowshoes have developed from the heavy wood and thick leather models, which were once standard gear for winter trappers, to high-tech, ultralight models used by backcountry trekkers, recreational walkers, and winter triathletes. If you can walk, you can snowshoe. It just takes some practice. It may seem a bit awkward at first, but the design of the shoes allows you to walk in a fairly normal gait. One difference between walking and snowshoeing is that you cannot go backward. The heel of the shoe will stick in the snow and you will find yourself quickly in the snow, rather than on it! So strap on a pair of snowshoes, dress in layers, and head out for a trek.

Snowshoeing Equipment

Shoes

Most modern snowshoes fall into three categories: mountaineering, recreational, and sport. Mountaineering snowshoes, also known as backcountry, backpacking, or hiking shoes, are for use on steep slopes and ice—where good traction, durability, and maneuverability are key. They have sophisticated bindings and large cleats on the bottom. These shoes tend to be the most costly as they are made of more durable, expensive materials.

Recreational shoes are also called walking or hiking shoes. These shoes are the scaled-down models of mountaineering snowshoes. They have less sophisticated bindings and are not suggested for use in extreme conditions that require added aggressive traction for steep slopes and ice. These are a good, all-around multipurpose shoe.

Sport snowshoes are also called running, racing, or crosstraining shoes and are the best type for use by multisport athletes. There are a few different styles of sport shoes, ranging from lighter versions of recreational models to highly specialized, smaller racing models designed for running races or winter triathlons on packed snow. Many of the sport shoes differ in shape from the traditional recreational and mountaineering snowshoes, which are symmetrical (the binding is placed in the center of each shoe). Sport models are asymmetrical, with the bindings mounted closer to the inside edge. This prevents the inside edges of the shoes hitting each other and enables you to take a more natural running stride.

Clothing
Follow the same guidelines used as when dressing for cross-country skiing.

Gaiters
These are a great plus to help keep snow out of your boots.

Ski Poles
Poles will help you keep your balance, work your upper body, and get up more easily when you fall.

HIKING

Hiking is a great off-season training option if you do not want to invest in the equipment needed for cross-country skiing or snowshoeing— or if you live in an area with little snow. All you need is a sturdy pair of trail shoes, access to trails, proper clothing, and a spirit for adventure. Depending on the terrain that you tackle, you can get in a solid aerobic hike or a thigh-busting anaerobic workout. Climbing steep hills will tax your aerobic system, building total lower-body strength, while downhill hiking will work your quadriceps and improve your balance.

As mentioned previously, hiking requires little equipment. However, utilizing two trekking poles is a new trend in hiking. These "ski-like" poles can help improve your momentum for uphill climbs, help relieve the stress on your knees during descents, and aid in balancing as you cross uneven terrain or streams. They will also work the muscles of the arms, shoulders, and upper back. These poles can be found at your local recreational outfitting store.

Depending upon the duration of your hike and its location, you will want to bring along some basic supplies. For short hikes (1–2 hours) close to home, a fanny pack with water and some energy bars will do the trick. It is okay to hike alone in familiar territory: Just make sure that you let someone know where you are going. However, for extended hikes in more remote areas, it is safest to bring along a friend or two and a daypack containing:

- Identification
- Map and compass
- Water and food
- Extra clothes and rain gear
- Cell phone
- Basic first-aid kit
- Pocketknife or multipurpose tool
- Matches in a waterproof container
- Sunscreen
- Prescribed medicines, such as an asthma inhaler or bee-sting kit

So strap on your trail shoes, head to your local park, or locate more extensive hiking trails through the national forest and park departments, and get out and enjoy the outdoors. A few hours on hiking trails is a great way to build your aerobic base, work on upper and lower body strength, and improve your balance while participating in a low-impact activity.

MOUNTAIN BIKING

Heading out to outdoor trails on your mountain bike is a great way to break up the monotony of indoor cycling during the winter months. You can go to your local greenway or to the wooded mountain bike trails that are found in most communities. When the temperature drops and the winter wind starts to blow, cycling in the woods gives you added shelter from the elements and allows you to get outdoors at a time when cycling on the open roads would be too uncomfortable. Mountain biking also helps you to build a smooth pedal stroke and greatly improves your bike handling. It takes great skill and concentration to ride your bike safely and effectively over rocks, roots, and loose soil; down steep, wooded descents; and up and over slick climbs. Learning to ride on such unpredictable and everchanging terrain will only enhance your road-handling skills come race season.

You can stick to flat or rolling terrain for a base-building endurance ride or head to the hills for a more difficult, heart-and-leg-busting effort. If you are new to the sport, see if you can find a beginners' clinic that you can attend, read a book that addresses technique for beginners, or head out with other seasoned riders and get some basic riding tips from them. Make sure that you start out on less technically demanding trails and gradually challenge yourself as you become more confident in your riding skills and abilities. Below is a list and description of some basic riding techniques that should help to get you started.

Mountain Biking Technique Recommendations

Balance

Balance is key in mountain biking—not only side to side, but also fore and aft. Keeping your weight over the rear wheel will give you traction. You need to find the proper balance to keep solid traction on the back wheel, while keeping the front wheel in contact with the ground. If you find that your front wheel is coming off the ground, then you need to transfer more weight to it.

Corner

Make sure you *brake before* the corners and then *accelerate out of them.* Look where you are going and lean into turns by keeping your inside knee up and out, while keeping firm pressure on the outside pedal.

Ascents

Different hill grades will require different climbing techniques and gear selections. Steep hill climbs will require you to ascend out of the saddle. Less steep hills will allow you to remain seated, "spinning" up the hill. With any terrain that looks beyond your ability, it is okay to get off your bike and walk, as reaching beyond your abilities can lead to possible injuries.

Descents
It is important to slide back on your saddle while descending. Often on steep descents, you may have to be completely behind the saddle. As mentioned previously in relation to corners, be sure to decrease your speed before heading into a corner and, as with climbing, do not descend anything that you question your ability to handle—when in doubt, dismount and walk.

Braking
Most of your braking force is in the front brake (it has about twice as much stopping power as the rear brake). Quick pressure to the front brake during a descent or even on the flats can send you flying over the handlebars. The safest braking technique is to begin applying the back brake and gradually introduce the front brake or use both brakes gently and in unison. Be sure to brake before corners, not in them. Locking your back brake to skid may seem like a neat maneuver, but it is damaging to the trail, is not particularly effective at slowing you down, and can cause you to lose control of your bike.

Shifting
Your gear selection should allow for a cadence range between 60 and 90 rpm. You will find that there is a greater range of lower gears on mountain bikes, enabling you to spin more, which is especially beneficial while riding on hilly terrain.

Single Track
These are narrow dirt trails on which there is not much room for error. Make sure that you keep looking forward, focusing on the trail ahead. Avoid looking off the trail, and be sure to slow down around blind curves (remember to brake prior to the curve)—it is hard to predict what lies ahead.

Mud
As noted in the IMBA Rules of the Trail, riding through mud can leave deep grooves, which in turn water follows, thus causing trail erosion.

If you must go through a muddy section on an otherwise dry trail, pull up lightly on the handlebars, and either keep up your speed or forge through. If the mud looks too deep, dismount and walk your bike around it.

Sand
Riding through sand has a similar feel to riding through mud. Sand tends to have a bit more give to it, so you might try a slightly higher gear than you would normally choose.

Streams and Other Water Areas
If possible, try not to ride through streams and other water areas. Repeated crossings can cause sedimentation of the stream and can lead to environmental damage. If you have no other option, maintain your speed through the water, pedaling in a low gear, keeping a gentle touch on the handlebars. Be sure to know the depth of the water before crossing!

Divots, Rocks, Holes, Roots, and Bumps
When going over uneven terrain that may trap your front wheel, you need to shift your weight back so that the front wheel can glide over the obstacles. If the obstacle is too high, you may need to pick up the front wheel to get over it, and generally your rear wheel should just roll through or up and over the obstacle. If in doubt as to whether or not you can make it over, dismount and carry your bike over the obstacle.

Mountain Biking Equipment
The following is a list of equipment and tools for mountain biking that you should always bring along with you before heading out on your own. Make sure that you are familiar with basic repair skills such as fixing a flat tire, replacing a derailed chain, fixing a broken chain, and tightening a loose spoke or replacing a broken spoke. If you are unfamiliar with these basic bike repairs, ask your local bike shop if they provide instruction or look for a book that covers repairs. You should already have the majority of the items listed; if not, all can be purchased at your local bike store, through a cycling catalog, or from an online store.

Helmet
This is the number-one piece of equipment that you must have before heading out the door, and your road bike helmet will work just fine.

Sunglasses
These are a must to protect your eyes from the sun, dust, dirt, bugs, and branches that you will encounter on the trail. Find a pair of glasses that have interchangeable lenses so that you can adapt to the different light levels during the day.

Seat Bag, Fanny Pack, or Backpack
Organize the equipment listed below, plus tools, extra clothing, and snacks into whichever bag you are the most comfortable with.

Pump
Make sure that the pump will fit your particular valve type (Schrader or Presta). There are many pumps on the market that are very compact, light, popular, and extremely efficient. Some will also adapt to any style of valve. They can be mounted on your bike or stuffed in your bag. You may also choose from one of many new CO_2 cartridge fillers on the market to lighten your load. The only drawback to these is that once the cartridge is empty, it is done, and if you have an additional flat and not enough cartridges, the long walk back to the car begins.

Spare Tube
It is easier and timelier to replace the tube while you are out on the trail and then repair the damaged tube when you get home. If you have room in your tool bag, you may want to carry more than one spare tube.

Patch Kit
Carry this in case you have more flats than tubes. It is a light, practical piece of back-up equipment.

Tire Irons
These come in various shapes, sizes, and materials and will help you take your tire off in order to change your tube.

Tools

Suggested tools include a small screwdriver, small crescent wrench, small metric wrenches, and assorted Allen wrenches. These tools can be used for various repairs and adjustments—from tweaking your derailleur, to removing a wheel that lacks a quick-release lever, to tightening a loose water bottle cage. They can be purchased separately, or you can look for a handy, compact, all-in-one tool.

Chain Tool

This is used for fixing a broken chain. If you do not have it or do not know how to use it, it could be a long walk back to your car. These will sometimes be found on the all-in-one tool.

Spoke Wrench

This tool is used for tightening loose spokes or removing broken ones.

Basic First-Aid Kit

With luck, this will not be necessary. But if you have a minor crash, you should be able cope with your injuries with materials in the basic kit until you can get professional care.

Water Bottles or Hydration System

Never venture out without an adequate supply of water or your favorite sports drink. Water bottles can be found at any cycling shop or sporting goods store, and there are many varieties of hydration systems from which to choose—from stand-alone systems to those built into a fanny pack or backpack.

Recommended Mountain Biking Clothing

The following clothing list will help make your ride safer and much more comfortable. Your clothing that you use for road cycling is easily interchangeable for mountain biking.

Gloves

These will keep your fingers and hands warm on cold days, provide cushioning for the palms of your hands to prevent blisters and nerve compression (which can lead to hand numbness), and, in the event of a fall, protect your skin from being torn up.

Padded Cycling Shorts
These are the same as used for road biking and help prevent chafing.

Cycling Jersey
These provide lots of pockets in which to stuff snacks, an extra water bottle, your jacket, cell phone, extra tubes, and more. Plus their usually bright colors will make you much more visible to other riders and users of the trails.

Windproof and/or Waterproof Jacket
This will help keep in warmth and protect you from the elements during the colder, wetter months of the off-season.

Mountain Bike Shoes
If you are a beginner, sturdy running shoes or trail shoes are an option. They will allow you to drop your feet quickly for balance in the case of a potential spill. After you become more confident with your riding abilities, you should switch to mountain bike shoes, which, due to their stiffer soles, will be more comfortable and provide much more efficient power transfer to the pedals. You will find many different brands and models to choose from, so check with your local bike shop on the correct pair for you.

Basic Mountain Bike Maintenance
Off-road cycling tends to be a bit messier than road cycling, and you will have to perform routine maintenance on your mountain bike to keep it operating smoothly and safely. Just as there are basic repairs that you should become familiar with, there are also basic maintenance jobs that you should be able to complete. For more involved tasks, take your bike to your local shop. The following is a brief list of things that you should be able to do at home and should already be familiar with from maintaining your road bike. Remember, performing these basic tasks will keep your bike in good operating condition and lessen the likelihood of a mid-ride breakdown that could result in a long, cold walk back to your car.

Chain Cleaning
A rag and some degreaser works well for this task, or you can purchase a chain-cleaning tool that can do the trick.

Keep the Chain Lubricated

There are many varieties of chain lubricant on the market. Find what you like and stick with it. Just be sure to wipe off the excess lubricant with a rag after you apply it.

Tire Pressure

Before every ride, check and properly inflate your tires. Check the sidewall of your tires for the recommended pressure.

Check the Headset

If it is loose, you will feel some "play," and it will need to be tightened. If you are unsure how to do this, or how much to tighten, take the bike to your local shop where they can adjust it properly for you.

Check the Brakes

Make sure that the brake pads are not rubbing on the rim and that the pads are not worn down.

Check Assorted Bolts

Constant bumping around on trails tends to loosen bolts more on mountain bikes than on road bikes. It is a good idea to check these frequently. Periodically, it is also a good idea to remove, grease, and replace the bolts. This prevents them from seizing into the frame and making them sometimes impossible to remove.

Check the Wheels

Make sure that the wheels are true (no wobbling) and that there are no loose or broken spokes. If the wheels are not spinning properly, you will need to take them to your local shop and have them trued.

Clean the Bike

A clean bike is a happy bike, and it is a good idea to perform a quick clean after every ride. Sometimes just a quick wipe down will do, and other times you may need to give it a more extensive wash, scrubbing off the day's mud. If you do break out the water, remember to dry off your bike completely and check to see if the cables, derailleurs, and chain need to be re-lubed.

IMBA RULES OF THE TRAIL

The following rules of the trail have been formulated by IMBA, the International Mountain Bicycling Association. These rules are recognized around the world as the standard code of conduct for mountain bikers. To make your and others' trips to the woods more enjoyable, you need to become familiar with these important rules of the trail.

Ride on Open Trails Only. Respect trail and road closures (ask if uncertain); avoid trespassing on private land; obtain permits or other authorization, as may be required. Federal and state wilderness areas are closed to cycling. The way you ride will influence trail management decisions and policies.

Leave No Trace. Be sensitive to the dirt beneath you. Recognize different types of soils and trail construction and practice low-impact cycling. Wet and muddy trails are more vulnerable to damage. When the trail-bed is soft, consider other riding options. This also means staying on existing trails and not creating new ones. Do not cut switchbacks. Be sure to pack out at least as much as you pack in.

Control Your Bicycle. Inattention for even a second can cause problems. Obey all bicycle speed regulations and recommendations.

Always Yield to Others on the Trail. Let your fellow trail users know you are coming. A friendly greeting or bell is considerate and works well—do not startle others. Show your respect when passing by, slowing to a walking pace or even stopping. Anticipate other trail users around corners or in blind spots. Yielding means slow down, establish communication, be prepared to stop, if necessary, and pass safely.

Never Scare Animals. An unannounced approach, a sudden movement, or a loud noise startles all animals. This can be dangerous for you, others, and the animals. Give animals extra room and time to adjust to you. When passing horses, use special care and follow directions from the horseback riders (ask if uncertain). Running cattle and disturbing wildlife is a serious offense. Leave gates as you found them, or as marked.

Plan Ahead. Know your equipment, your ability, and the area in which you are riding and prepare accordingly. Be self-sufficient at all times, keep your equipment in good repair, and carry necessary supplies for changes in weather or other conditions. A well-executed trip is a satisfaction to you and not a burden to others. Always wear a helmet and appropriate safety gear.

CYCLO-CROSS

Another terrific option that can add variety to your training during the fall and early winter months is cyclo-cross. This is a sport that has been around since the early 1900s, when European nations began holding championships. (The first world championships were held in Paris in 1950.) It is a much newer sport in the United States, having only been around for the last 20 years or so. It is a sport that combines the endurance of a triathlete, the running skills of a duathlete, the bike-handling skills of a mountain biker, and the power and finesse of a road racer.

9.1

During the months of October through December, you are apt to find an event in your area every weekend. Races are generally held at public parks or school campuses, and the course can traverse a wide variety of surfaces, including paved paths, paved and gravel roads, parking lots, fields, and trails. The terrain is fairly wide open, which allows for safe passing and great spectator viewing. Courses usually are a one- to one-and-a-half-mile loop that presents the riders with sharp turns, gullies, hills, obstacles, hurdles, and steps. Some of the obstacles (natural and man-made) require you to dismount, pick up your bike, and carry it up and over the physical barriers.

The inclusion of cyclo-cross racing to your off-season training program can provide you with the motivation to train during the cold and wet fall and winter months, improve your bike-handling skills, and offer you a fun, active, and social way to spend the weekend. Because cyclo-cross racing is a high-intensity workout that will most likely have you at or above threshold for the duration of the event, you need to build it into your training plan cautiously (with appropriate rest and recovery). It is a sport of transitions and speed changes, balance and toughness—a wet and slippery version of the 40K bike leg of a triathlon.

There are generally five races per day, and they last about 1 hour for the elites and 30 to 45 minutes for the other categories. The categories include races for beginners (C), intermediates (B), and experts (A), which offer age and gender breakdowns (juniors under 23 and master's categories for 35+, 45+, and 55+ competitors). There is also an open category called "senior" that has no age limits, and some races will offer special kid's races—fun for the entire family.

Recommended Cyclo-Cross Equipment

Most bike shops now carry stock cyclo-cross bikes, and prices range from about $800 for an entry-level bike to well over $2,500 for a top-of-the-line model. They look similar to road bikes, except the frames are a bit beefier, the tires knobby and wider, and the brakes are cantilevered (cantilevered brakes allow for more clearance over the tires to deal with the mud and other debris on the course).

If you are not ready to add yet another bike to your stable, you can convert an old road bike or use a mountain bike. The easiest and least costly option would be to use your mountain bike, stripped of everything that you do not need—water bottle cages, pump, saddlebag, bar ends, and so on. If you want to do more to adapt your mountain bike, change the tires and select as small a tire profile as the rims will accept. This will increase the bike's rolling resistance, while giving you a bit more tire clearance. Converting a road bike will take a bit more time and money, because you will have to change your brake and pedal systems, add knobby tires and, as with the mountain bike, remove all non-essential add-ons.

Recommended Cyclo-Cross Clothing

Your regular winter riding attire should allow you to accommodate the rigors of cyclo-cross racing. Just make sure that all of your clothing fits snugly. Loose clothing can get easily hung up on the bike as you are dismounting and mounting, which will either slow you or knock you down. Be prepared for all types of weather and carry a variety of clothing layers with you to the race. Most importantly, do not forget your helmet. Depending upon your pedal system, flexible mountain bike shoes (stiff mountain bike shoes or shoes with carbon fiber soles will not be very comfortable) or trail shoes with good traction will work fine. There are specific crosstraining shoes now on the market and they have a flexible toe, which is better suited for running off the bike, and removable soccer-type cleats at the toe to provide better traction on muddy courses.

7 TIPS TO MAKE YOUR CYCLO-CROSS TRAINING AND RACING EXPERIENCE A SUCCESS

Rest—Cross racing is a short but extremely intense activity, and it is key that you include enough rest and recovery in between your hard training sessions and racing. Including just one hard effort during the week along with races on the weekends will maintain your sharpness for cross-racing without sacrificing your overall fitness goals for the off-season. Do not wear yourself out.

Work on Your Technique—Make sure to practice your starts, dismounts, mounts, and run-ups. Include at least one technique workout on your cross bike each week to improve your transition from on-the-bike riding to off-the-bike running.

Know the Course—Make sure that you ride the course a few times prior to the start. Complete a few slow laps, noting the difficult sections, and practice your dismount, mounts, and run-ups. Make your final lap before you head to the starting line a bit more intense so that you are thoroughly warmed up and ready for the start.

Have a Race Plan—Be prepared by knowing if you are going to get out quick on the start or take the more cautious route and let the others clear out of the way. Getting out quickly will prevent you from a getting stuck behind a potential bottleneck if the trail gets too narrow or there is a crash. Just make sure that you are able to keep up the pace! Know when and where you can make a productive move to gain on, overtake, or distance yourself from the competition and where you can get a breather (if any).

Check Your Equipment—Make sure that your tires have the right amount of air pressure in them—this will depend on the conditions and

Cyclo-Cross Technique Recommendations

Dismounts, running with your bike, and remounts are the three key techniques that you will have to practice to become an efficient cyclo-cross rider. These can be the areas in the race where you can either make up some time—if you have mastered these techniques, or waste precious energy and time, if carried out improperly. They take lots of practice to master, so start out on a smooth grassy surface, and as you become more confident, perform these maneuvers on progressively more challenging surfaces.

the type of course. Your pre-race warm-up on the course will give you an opportunity to test different pressures and see what feels best. Be familiar with the terrain at the start and be sure to adjust your gearing so that you are in the appropriate chain ring at the start. Be sure to clean and lubricate your bike (check the mountain bike section) after each race or messy training session.

Be Well Fueled—You should already have removed the water bottle cages from your bike. Since the race will last no more than an hour, hydrating during the event is not a priority. It is key, however that you fuel well before the event. A high-carbohydrate breakfast of about 300 calories, along with at least twelve ounces of water at least 2 hours prior to the event, should do. Also, during the drive to the race and during your warm-up, you should attempt to consume at least twelve ounces of your favorite sports drink and then just sip on water about 20 minutes out from the start. If you have a friend who is tagging along with you to the race to cheer you on, he or she is allowed to hand a water bottle off to you if necessary. It is also a priority, especially due to the intense nature of the event, to refuel immediately following the race. Proper consumption (within 30 minutes of the event) of a recovery drink containing a 4:1 (carbohydrate to protein) ratio will replace expended glycogen and electrolytes, provide protein for tissue regeneration, rehydrate you, and curb your hunger.

Have Fun—Remember that you are competing in cyclo-cross racing to supplement and to add some variety to your off-season training. Be smart while you are racing and do not take any unnecessary risks just to "catch that guy or girl ahead." Treat your races as "C" priority, be safe, and go out and enjoy the day.

Dismounts

As you approach a dismount area on the course, place your hands on the tops of your bars or brake hoods, have your left pedal down, take your right foot from its pedal, and then swing your right leg over the rear wheel. Bring your right leg forward between your left leg and the frame, while moving your right hand to the top tube just in front of the seat post. Just as your right foot is about to hit the ground, remove your left foot from its pedal, putting your weight on your right arm and hit the ground running (your left hand is still holding onto the bars). See the next section for running with the bike.

For a dismount over a barrier, begin as above, maintain your grip on the handle bars with your left hand (this will keep the front wheel straight) and lift the bike with your right hand, which is on the top-tube, and hurdle the barrier.

Running with Your Bike

Once you have dismounted and are running, hoist the bike up onto your shoulder (find a good balance point along the top tube to rest the bike). Then position your right arm around the head tube and grab the left brake hood (this will keep the front wheel from wobbling around while you run). To put the bike back on the ground, hold onto the bars with your left hand and take the bike off your shoulder with your right hand, either by the top or down tube. Make sure that you set it down gently to make your remount easier.

Remounts

Once the bike has made contact with the ground, move your right hand to the bars and leap off of your left foot, throwing your right leg over the saddle, then landing on the inside of your right thigh and sliding onto the saddle. Find your pedals quickly, first the right (the pedal should be around 12 o'clock from a proper dismount) and then the left as the pedal rotates.

SUGGESTED CYCLO-CROSS WORKOUTS

WORKOUT 1: Technique Session

On your cross bike, warm up with some easy riding for 15 to 20 minutes, on or off the road. During the last 5 minutes of your warm-up, include several 20-second accelerations with easy-spin rest intervals. Then on a grassy area, practice your starting line starts—start from a standstill, sprint for 15 to 20 seconds, spin easy for recovery, and repeat. After several of these sprint starts, practice smooth and efficient dismounts and mounts. You can also add barriers that you will need to dismount for, pick up your bike, run over, and remount. One final aspect that you need to address is run-ups. Find a hill or set of steps and practice dismounting and running up with your bike on your shoulder. Mount at the top, ride back down, and repeat several times. End your technical session with an easy spin cool-down. This session should last for an hour.

WORKOUT 2: Crisscross Session

This high-intensity workout mirrors the intensity that you will achieve during a race and can be completed on road, cross, or mountain bike. First, warm up as in the previous session. Then perform several sets of 2 to 4 minutes of hard efforts (above your Lactate Threshold or LT), with 5 minutes of easy spinning between sets. The total "work" portion of the workout should be between 20 and 30 minutes, and the total session should last 45 minutes to 1 hour. Make sure that you include at least a 10-minute easy spin at the end for a cool-down.

WORKOUT 3: Steady-State Session

This workout can also be completed on your road, cross, or mountain bike. After a 15- to 20-minute warm-up, build your effort to just below your LT and maintain this pace for 5 to 20 minutes (this all depends on your current level of fitness). Cool down with an easy spin. This workout should last between 45 minutes to 1 hour.

Cyclo-cross training and racing can be a great addition to your off-season training. All you really need to do is to include one cyclo-cross technique workout each week, along with one intense bike workout (these could even be combined into one workout, using the technique session as a warm-up to the more intense work), in addition to your regular off-season swim/bike/run routine. Focus on the fun, social aspects of this down-and-dirty activity, and you will find yourself coming into your triathlon season mentally tougher, physically stronger, and with greatly enhanced bike-handling skills.

RESOURCES

CROSS-COUNTRY SKIING

www.crosscountryskier.com—This is a great Web site, offering travel information, gear reviews and advice, ski instruction, industry news, and related links.

www.xcskiworld.com—The largest English-language cross-country Web site; contains great training tips for beginners.

SNOWSHOEING

www.atlassnowshoe.com—This site contains a brief history of snowshoes, guide to modern snowshoes, advice on selection, plus a list of dealers from the Atlas Snowshoe maker.

HIKING

www.onedayhikes.com—This is a Web site dedicated to finding one-day hikes or walks anywhere in the world.

MOUNTAIN BIKING

www.imba.com—The official site for the International Mountain Biking Association.

www.mountainbike.com—This is a great site for gear news and reviews, bike tests, race results, and a trail finder.

www.mtb.liv.com—This is a site that helps you find places to ride in the United States and around the world and also contains information on races and events.

CYCLO-CROSS

www.cylcocrossworld.com—A Web site touted as "All cross all the time."

www.worldcycling.com—A Web site that includes a great selection of cyclo-cross race videos.

Off the Road—A complete video technical guide to off-road riding from the British Cyclo-Cross Association, written by Martin Eadon, a former national cyclo-cross champion, available from the British Cyclo-Cross Association, 14 Deneside Road, Darlington Co. Durham, DL 39HZ Tel/Fax 01325482052.

R E F E R E N C E S

Burke, Edmund R. *Off-Season Training for Cyclists.* Boulder, CO: VeloPress, 1997.

Burney, Simon. *Cyclo-Cross Training and Technique.* 2nd ed. Boulder, CO: VeloPress, 1996.

Friel, Joe. *The Mountain Biker's Training Bible: A Complete Training Guide for the Competitive Mountain Biker.* Boulder, CO: VeloPress, 2000.

Peterson, Paul, John Morton, and Rick Lovett. *The Essential Cross-Country Skier: A Step-By-Step Guide.* Cambden, ME: Ragged Mountain Press, 1999.

Scheve, Inge. "Cross-Country Skiing, An Introduction to the Art." RaceCenter Northwest, February/March 2003, 30–32.

USA Cycling Coaching Staff. *USA Cycling Sport Coach Manual.* Colorado Springs, CO: USA Cycling, Inc., 1999.

10 Strength Training:

OFF-SEASON OPTIONS

You should look at strength training as a supplement to your regular training regimen, and the off-season is the perfect time to head back to the gym to gain and then maintain strength. There are many different strength training programs you can follow that offer various benefits and take differing commitments of time. This chapter will briefly discuss several different phases of strength training that you can incorporate comfortably into your off-season schedule. These are only guidelines, and it is recommended that you consult a certified trainer to teach you the proper form for each exercise. There are also many books and videos available that contain detailed photos or illustrations that can help you perform the exercises properly.

Please note that core exercises are not included in this strength training section and have been discussed fully in Chapter 3. You can add the core sessions to the same day that you strength train, or they may be stand-alone sessions. You will need to choose whichever best suits your individual training needs.

STRENGTH TRAINING PHASES

Anatomical Adaptation (AA)

This is the beginning phase of your strength training program in which you are preparing your tendons and muscles for the increased weight loads of the upcoming phases. It is typically incorporated in the Preparation and Base I phases, and the sessions should be carried out two to three times per week.

WORKOUT 1: **Anatomical Adaptation**

Frequency: 2–3 times per week

Phase Length: 4–8 weeks

Equipment: Body weight, free weights, machines, or any combination of the three

Load: Choose a weight that will allow you to complete 20–30 repetitions.

Sets: 3–5 (dependent upon the amount of time you have)

Reps: 20–30

Rest Interval: 60–90 seconds between sets, or you can complete this workout as circuit, moving right from one exercise to the next (alternate upper- and lower-body exercises)

Speed: Slow, focusing on perfect form

Progression: When you reach three sets of thirty reps, increase the load in small increments.

Exercises: Complete one set of each exercise in the order listed below and then repeat the order for the next set. The load for the first set should be lightest of the session.

1. Hip extension (squat—can be one- or two-leg, step-up, leg press, or walking lunge)

2. Standing straight-arm lat pull-down or seated lat pull-down with palms facing you

3. Hip extension different than the one in #1

4. Dumbbell chest press or push-ups (these can be done while on a Swiss ball)

5. Seated row or standing one-arm row

6. Calf raise—single or both legs

Max Transition (MT)

This focuses on building strength gradually, rather than jumping into a full maximum strength session. (If you are an experienced lifter you may want to focus on max lifts.) This phase allows for safer strength gains and faster recovery time than the max strength phase, relying on moderate loads and repetitions. MT can be carried out in Base II and III and should be completed two times per week.

WORKOUT 2: **Max Transition**

Frequency: 2 times per week

Phase Length: 4–8 weeks

Equipment: Body weight, free weights, machines, or any combination of the three

Load: Choose a weight that will allow you to complete 10–15 repetitions (10–12 for upper-body exercises and 12–15 for lower-body exercises). The load for the first set should be the lightest of the session. Once you attain the highest repetition while maintaining perfect form, increase your load slightly.

Sets: 3–4 (dependent upon the amount of time you have)

Reps: 10–15

Rest Interval: 1.5–3 minutes between sets

Speed: Slow to moderate, focusing on perfect form

Progression: Complete all sets of each exercise before moving on to the next exercise listed below.

Exercises: These are performed in the order listed.
1. Hip extension (squat—can be one- or two-leg, step-up, leg press, or walking lunge)
2. Standing straight-arm lat pull-down or seated lat pull-down with palms facing you
3. Dumbbell chest press or push-ups (these can be done while on a Swiss ball)
4. Seated row or standing one-arm row
5. Calf raise—single or both legs

Power Endurance (PE)

This strength training phase utilizes moderately fast, controlled movements that focus on building the explosive power needed for climbing short, steep hills or for short sprints to get ahead of a swim pack. This phase can be carried out in the Base II or III phase, depending on how long you stuck with the MT phase, and should be completed two times per week.

WORKOUT 3: Power Endurance

Frequency: 2 times per week

Phase Length: 2–6 weeks

Equipment: Body weight, free weights, machines, or any combination of the three

Load: Choose a weight that will allow you to complete 8–15 repetitions (lower reps for the upper-body exercises and higher for the lower-body exercises. The load for the first set should be the lightest of the session. Increase your load slightly once you attain the highest repetition, while maintaining perfect form.

Sets: 2–4 (dependent upon the amount of time you have)

Reps: 8–15

Rest Interval: 3–5 minutes between sets

Speed: Upward movements are quick, but controlled, and downward movements are slow and controlled.

Progression: Complete all sets of each exercise before moving on to the next exercise listed below.

Exercises: These are performed in the order listed.
1. Hip extension (squat, step-up, or leg-press)
2. Standing straight-arm lat pull-down or seated lat pull-down with palms facing you
3. Dumbbell chest press or push-ups—follow the MT phase guidelines
4. Seated row or standing one-arm row
5. Calf raise—follow the MT phase guidelines

Strength Maintenance (SM)

This is carried out one time per week and is used to maintain the strength gained during the previous phases. It should not be a taxing workout, and you should be able to complete the session in about an hour.

WORKOUT 4: Strength Maintenance

Frequency: 1 time per week

Phase Length: Dependent upon the length of your competitive season

Equipment: Body weight, free weights, machines, or any combination of the three

Load: Choose a weight that will allow you to complete six to twelve repetitions. Lighter load on the first one or two sets and heavier on the last.

Sets: 2–3 (dependent upon the amount of time you have) Complete 12 reps on the first one or two sets and 6–12 reps for the last set.

Reps: 6–12

Rest Interval: 1–2 minutes between sets

Speed: Slow to moderate, focusing on perfect form

Progression: Complete all sets of each exercise before moving on to the next exercise.

Exercises: These are performed in the order listed.

1. Hip extension (squat—can be one- or two-leg, step-up or walking lunge)
2. Standing straight-arm lat pull-down or seated lat pull-down with palms facing you
3. Dumbbell chest press or push-ups (these can be done while on a Swiss ball)
4. Seated row or standing one-arm row
5. Calf raise—single or both legs

STRENGTH TRAINING TIPS

- If uncertain about the correct way to perform an exercise, seek qualified assistance.

- Maintain perfect form throughout the entire movement.

- Never sacrifice perfect form to lift added weight.

- Focus on the large muscle groups that will be utilized during swimming, cycling, and running.

- If possible, while carrying out the exercise, mimic the movement of the joint(s) that you will be using while you swim, bike, and run.

- To maximize your time, try to choose exercises that utilize multi-joints rather than just focusing on one joint movement.

- Estimate your load conservatively, slowly increasing the load until you hit the prescribed number of repetitions listed for each phase.

- Allow at least 48 hours between sessions.

- Warm up prior to each session for about 5 to 10 minutes (easy run, spin, elliptical trainer, stair-climber, rower).

- Cool down after each session with about 5 to 10 minutes of easy spinning on a bike or walking on a treadmill.

REFERENCES

Bernhardt, Gale. *Training Plans for Multisport Athletes.* Boulder, CO: VeloPress, 2000.

Crowley, Tim. "Functional Strength Training for Triathletes." www.ridefast. com/page. asp?page_id=content&page_content=A-8&CategoryID =80&ArticleID=29#article

Friel, Joe. *The Triathlete's Training Bible.* 2nd ed. Boulder, CO: VeloPress, 2004.

Niederpruem, Mike. "How Can You Resist? Resistance Training Can Be a Powerful Off-Season Tool." www.ridefast.com/page.asp?page_id= content&page_content=A-8&CategoryID=66&ArticleID=31#article

APPENDIX A

Goal-Setting Worksheet

G O A L 1 _____

LIMITER _____

TRAINING OBJECTIVES

1 _____

2 _____

3 _____

4 _____

G O A L 2 _____

LIMITER _____

TRAINING OBJECTIVES

1 _____

2 _____

3 _____

4 _____

G O A L 3 _____

LIMITER _____

TRAINING OBJECTIVES

1 _____

2 _____

3 _____

4 _____

APPENDIX B

Off-Season Training Plan Worksheets

OFF-SEASON TRAINING PLAN WORKSHEET: 16 WEEKS

WEEK	RACES	PERIOD	HOURS	
1				
2				
3				
4				
5				
6				
7				
8				
9				
10				
11				
12				
13				
14				
15				
16				

	SWIM					BIKE					RUN					
	E	F	S	ME	T	E	F	S	ME	T	E	F	S	ME	T	WTS

OFF-SEASON TRAINING PLAN WORKSHEET: 20 WEEKS

WEEK	RACES	PERIOD	HOURS	
1				
2				
3				
4				
5				
6				
7				
8				
9				
10				
11				
12				
13				
14				
15				
16				
17				
18				
19				
20				

	SWIM					BIKE					RUN					
	E	F	S	ME	T	E	F	S	ME	T	E	F	S	ME	T	WTS

APPENDIX C

Sample Off-Season Training Plan: 500 Annual Hours

SAMPLE OFF-SEASON TRAINING PLAN: 500 ANNUAL HOURS

WEEK	RACES	PERIOD	HOURS	
1		PREP	8.5	
2		PREP	8.5	
3		PREP	8.5	
4		PREP	8.5	
5		B-I	10	
6		B-I	12	
7		B-I	13.5	
8		B-I	7	
9		B-II	10.5	
10		B-II	12.5	
11		B-II	14	
12	"C" Masters swim meet: mile and 500 events	B-II	6.5	
13		B-III	11	
14	"C" 10K road race	B-III	13.5	
15		B-III	15	
16		B-III	7	

KEY: PREP = preparation   B-I = Base I   B-II = Base II   B-III = Base III

SWIM					BIKE					RUN					WTS
E	F	S	ME	T	E	F	S	ME	T	E	F	S	ME	T	
X		X	X	X	X		X		X	X		X		X	AA
X		X			X		X			X		X			AA
X		X			X		X			X		X			AA
X		X	X	X	X		X		X	X		X		X	AA
X		X			X		X			X		X			MT
X		X			X		X			X		X			MT
X		X			X		X			X		X			MT
X		X			X		X			X		X			MT
X	X	X	X	X	X	X	X	X	X	X	X	X	X	X	MT
X	X	X	X		X	X	X	X		X	X	X	X		MT
X	X	X	X		X	X	X	X		X	X	X	X		MT
X		X			X		X			X		X			PE
X	X	X	X	X	X	X	X	X	X	X	X	X	X	X	PE
X	X	X	X		X	X	X	X		X	X	X	X		PE
X	X	X	X		X	X	X	X		X	X	X	X		PE
X		X			X		X			X		X			PE

APPENDIX D

Testing Protocols

SWIM TIME TRIAL IN THE POOL

This test will give you your 100 yard/meter pace that you can later use to base your swim workouts on. This pace is often called your "T-Pace." It is best to approach the time trial as if it were a race day. This means that the few days prior to the test should have been relatively easy days of training and that you should be race-day fueled the day of the test.

The test is completed in a 25-yard/meter pool. After a short warm-up, start your stopwatch and swim 1,000 yards/meters at a steady pace ("race effort"). Stop your watch at the end of the time trial and note your finish time. Make sure that you get in an easy cooldown swim following the time trial. It is not necessary to use your heart rate monitor for this test, as they often do not read accurately in the water.

On your testing result sheet (Appendix E) enter the date and time of your test and record your 1,000 yard/meter time and your average 100 yard/meter time. To determine your 100 yard/meter time, divide your finish time by 10 and then convert the time to minutes and seconds (18 minutes divided by 10 equals 1.8, which equals 1 minute, 48 seconds—1:48 per 100). If you do choose to wear your heart rate monitor and can get a good reading, you can also note your average and max heart rate.

BIKE TIME TRIAL

This test will help you determine your lactate threshold (LT) heart rate, and that number can be used to determine your heart rate training zones. It is best to approach the time trial as if it were a race day. This means that the few days prior to the test should have been relatively easy days of training and that you should be race-day fueled the day of the test.

Find a flat, safe section of road that you can complete a 30-minute out-and-back time trial on. Warm up prior to the 30-minute effort and then start your heart rate monitor. Ten minutes into the test, hit your lap button, and then stop the monitor after 20 minutes. The number that you are interested in is the average heart rate of the last 20 minutes of the test. Also note your distance covered and max heart rate and enter this data on your testing result sheet.

This test may also be completed on a trainer or CompuTrainer. Just be sure to be consistent with the resistance setting on the trainer and the calibration of the CT. If completed on a CT or another device that measures power output, such as a PowerTap or SRM, note your average and max watts for the 30-minute effort.

RUN TIME TRIAL

This run test will help you determine your lactate threshold (LT) heart rate, and that number can be used to determine your heart rate training zones. It is best to approach the time trial as if it were a race day. This means that the few days prior to the test should have been relatively easy days of training and that you should be race-day fueled the day of the test.

Find a flat, safe section of road that you can complete a 30-minute out-and-back time trial on.

Warm up prior to the 30-minute effort and then start your heart rate monitor. Ten minutes into the test, hit your lap button, and then stop the monitor after 20 minutes. The number that you are interested in is the average heart rate for the last 20 minutes of the test. Also note your distance covered and max heart rate and enter this data on your testing result sheet.

This test can also be completed on a track, which should enable you to measure the distance more easily.

APPENDIX E

Testing Results Worksheet

TESTING RESULTS WORKSHEET

DATE	SPORT	TEST	DISTANCE	TIME	

	AVERAGE HEART RATE	MAXIMUM HEART RATE	PACE	AVERAGE WATTS	MAXIMUM WATTS

APPENDIX F

Sample Testing Results Worksheet

SAMPLE TESTING RESULTS WORKSHEET

DATE	SPORT	TEST	DISTANCE	TIME	
2/6/05	Running	30-min. time trial	5 miles	30:00	
2/9/05	Cycling	30-min. time trial	10.5 miles	30:00	
2/12/05	Swimming	Time trial	1,000 yards	15:20	

AVERAGE HEART RATE	MAXIMUM HEART RATE	PACE	AVERAGE WATTS	MAXIMUM WATTS
162	195	6:00/mile		
153	187	21 mph	176	201
		1:32/100 yd		

Workout Codes

AA	Anatomical Adaptation
CT	CompuTrainer
CW	Core Work
DWR	Deep-Water Running
E	Endurance—These workouts consist of steady-state, low-effort work.
ET	Elliptical Trainer
F	Force/hill—These workouts include hilly runs and rides, open-water swims, and hill interval repeats.
FG	Fixed Gear Bike
LT	Lactate Threshold
MB	Mountain Bike
ME	Muscular Endurance—These workouts include tempo work (steady-state work, up to Zone 3) and cruise intervals (4 to 6 minutes long, up to Zone 4).
MT	Max Transition
PC	PowerCranks
PE	Power Endurance
R	Recovery—Very low-effort workouts that help produce a recovery effect.
RE	Rowing Ergometer
S	Form/drill—These workouts include exercises that focus on various aspects of a specific sport.
SB	Spin Bike
SC	Stair-Climber
SM	Strength Maintenance
SS	Snowshoeing
T	Testing—This workout determines your 100 yard/meter pace or your heart rate training zones.
TM	Treadmill

WTS	Weights
XB	Cross Bike
XC	Cross-Country Skiing
XT	Crosstraining—This category implies other workouts than swim/bike/run/strength/core.
Y	Yoga

Glossary

A, B, and C Races. The ranking of importance of races, with A being the highest priority and C the lowest.

Base Phase. The main phase of training prior to your race-specific build.

Build Phase. The specific phase of training during which high-intensity training is introduced, focusing on the development of muscular endurance, speed endurance, and power—while maintaining endurance, force, and speed.

Endurance. The ability of the body to resist fatigue. Also a category of workout listed in this book.

Force. The strength evident in a muscle while exerting against a resistance. Also a category of workout listed in this book.

Glycogen. The form in which glucose is stored in the muscles and liver.

Lactate. A substance formed when lactic acid from within the cells enters the bloodstream.

Lactate Threshold. The point during exercise where increasing intensity causes blood lactate levels to accumulate.

Limiters. Specific weaknesses within a particular sport that can be holding you back from achieving a goal.

Macrocycle. A large block of training time, usually an entire year.

Medicine Ball. A weighted exercise ball.

Microcycle. A smaller block of training time, usually one week.

Mitochondrial Volume. The amount of mitochondria, energy production sites, within the muscles.

Muscular Endurance. The ability of a muscle to perform repeated contractions for a long period of time. Also a category of workout listed in this book.

Off-Season. The important period of time in your training schedule between your last race and when you begin specific training for the next season.

Power. The ability to apply force in an efficient manner.

Repetitions (Reps). The number of times a certain movement is repeated.

Set. A group of repetitions for a particular exercise.

Speed Skill. The ability to move the body in an efficient manner. Also a category of workout listed in this book.

Strokes Per Minute (SPM). The number of row strokes taken per minute while on a rowing machine.

Swiss Ball. Also called a stability or physio ball; used to perform specific exercises.

Training Objectives. A list of training marks to meet to achieve a certain goal.

Transition Phase. A period of unstructured training prior to the base phase.

Ventilatory Threshold (VT). This is the point where, during increasing exertion, breathing first becomes labored. VT closely corresponds with lactate threshold.

VO_2max. The capacity for oxygen consumption by the body during maximal exertion. Also known as aerobic capacity and max oxygen consumption.

Index

About the Author

K aren Buxton has been involved in coaching for over eighteen years—working with athletes at every level, from youth basketball to college soccer to elite multisport. Karen, who has a B.S. from Johnson State College and an M.Ed. in athletic administration from Temple University, holds coaching certifications of Level-II from USA Triathlon and Expert-Level from USA Cycling. She also has served as the Secretary-General of USA Triathlon's board of directors.

A competitive athlete herself, Karen comes from a background that includes playing on her boys' high school soccer team and being a Division I Alpine skier. In addition to these two sports, she competed at both the high school and college levels on varsity teams in basketball, field hockey, softball, tennis, and rugby. She was also inducted into both her high school and college athletic halls of fame.

Taking up triathlon twelve years ago, Karen has worked her way from a mid-packer in sprint-distance races to representing the United States on nine world teams (four in triathlon and five in duathlon). Over the past several years, she has shifted her competitive focus to ultra-distance events, including five ironman-distance races and a fifth place overall finish in the 2000 U.S. Long Course Championships.

The high point of her ultra-distance racing career (so far) took place in June 2002, when Karen's four-woman team won their category in the 3,000-mile Race Across America (RAAM), cycling from Portland, OR, to Pensacola, FL, in just over seven days.

Karen brings a wealth of personal competitive experience to her coaching. And as a wife and mother of two young teenage children, she is aware of the delicate balance required to develop a satisfying athletic commitment within the day-to-day essential framework of her clients' busy lives. Karen, who lives in Greensboro, North Carolina, is a Joe Friel Ultrafit Coaching Associate and can be reached through her Web site at www.coachbuxton.com.